Wouldn't Be Fittin'

A Memoir of Custom and Costume in the Changing South

By Douglas Haas-Bennett
and J. Griffin Hughes

Dedicated with deepest gratitude to the Haas and Bennett families and the extended family of Raleigh Creative Costumes.

Contents

Prologue

My parents met Miss Doug as part of the Raleigh community theater scene, and the summer that I was to turn twenty-one, Dad asked her if I could work at her shop, Raleigh Creative Costumes. So I met her as many other young people have, seeing her as part of my parents' life before me, one of those adult figures that we so easily take for granted when we are just beginning to become adults ourselves.

She addressed me in a courteous manner that I took to be the standard, stiff formality of old people and authority in general. I did not then understand the cultural legacy represented by the gentility of her demeanor, how it marked her as daughter of the landed gentry, the aristocracy of the Old South. This was the New South I was growing up in, and I did not recognize its roots any more than a fish knows the color of water.

While I never had much of a Southern accent, hers reminded me of my grandmother's, not the harsh country twang heard on *Hee-Haw* or coming from the *Simpson's* character Cletus the Slack-Jawed Yokel. It has a steady, silken quality to it. Vowels elongate for emphasis. Soft consonants are dwelt upon as if being savored, bringing to mind the sweetness of our native cuisine—crisp iced tea on a hot summer day, succulent collard greens braised with pork fat, ripe watermelon juices dripping down the chin.

I wasn't a very good employee at the time, and Miss Doug tolerated me graciously. After undertaking a long project of sorting and inventorying several dusty bookcases of playscripts for sale, I spent some time organizing shelves of rubber animal noses, cake make-up, latex prosthetics, spirit gum, mint-flavored blood, and hats for sailors, soldiers, and cowboys; walls of fairy wands and wings, plastic swords and pitchforks, beards and wigs for old men, fancy ladies, presidents, and hippies, and masks for robots, aliens, and Mardi Gras; bins full of tribal beads, hobo teeth, plastic jewelry, and bullwhips; racks of silver-trimmed angel robes, bat-wing-edged vampire capes, shimmering and lacy princess dresses, brightly colored clown overalls, pin-striped mobster suits, pleather Roman centurion armor, and depictions of odd-ball characters like the Monopoly guy and the father of a family who had batteries in their backs from a series of 1990s TV commercials.

But after a while, I could not find much to do to earn my eight-dollars-an-hour. Summer brought few customers, school plays being the primary draw to the shop outside of Halloween. The office manager sat at her desk, working on the accounts. Seamstresses worked in the back, preparing and repairing costumes as old as I was and older. Other sales staff came in and out on different days of the week. Doug herself would be at her computer and often stepping out to see an old friend or have her weekly visit to the hair salon. I eventually gave up on productivity and brought books to work. I would read for most of the day, sometimes the whole day, not doing much more than taking up space and waiting for a customer.

That was why, when I heard Doug call out to me to come see her in the office, I was pretty sure I was about to get yelled at, maybe even told that they didn't need me at the shop anymore. But then I rounded the corner and saw the room filled with aliens, all with the same blank oval faces and the same large black eyes, some white and some the greenish hue of glow-in-the-dark plastic, wearing the same silver capes, some taller, some shorter, some thicker, some thinner, sitting and standing.

Prologue

Someone turned on the opening theme tune from *The X-Files*. The movie of that TV show had just come out that summer, and the rest of the staff knew I was a fan. I'd even made up a window display with two mannequins as the main characters and a third dressed as a fish-headed creature.

My alien-masked co-workers began to drone along tunelessly with the music, "Happy birthday to you... Happy birthday to you..." Chills overcame me. I couldn't make a sound. On some instinctual level, it was terrifying. And it was beautiful. I didn't know they even knew it was my birthday. I never thought they would be putting in this kind of effort for me. They handed me an alien mask to wear myself, like they had landed on Earth to take me back home with them as one of their own.

When finally I could speak again, and masks were removed and cheers replaced droning, Doug brought out a bottle of champagne and showed me how to remove the cork without injury to life, limb, or property and how to pour a glass so the bubbles did not overwhelm it. That was my first legal drink, there in the office where I had once found a bottle of whiskey in the "Jimmy Thiem Memorial Drawer" of the filing cabinet, named for a deceased local celebrity and costume shop employee. A black and white photo of Jimmy Thiem himself, in old-age stage make-up for one of his stage roles, looked down at us as we sipped champagne and spread cheese onto crackers.

This was how Raleigh Creative Costumes celebrated everyone's birthday and sometimes other special events. Later, to welcome Doug back from a trip around the time of the theatrical release of *Titanic,* we greeted her at the door wearing period costumes of the doomed ship's passengers and sang her the first lines of the Celine Dion song, "Near... Far... Wherever you are!" before I ran into the room dressed as the iceberg in a sharply pointed white powdered wig, an angel's robe stretched out over a Southern Belle's hoop skirt, and frosty blue face make-up to knock all of the other employees down. Doug loved the bit so much she made us do it a second time.

At the end of my first summer at the shop, I went back to school but returned to work weekends in September, when the Halloween season started up. After Halloween, I returned again over Christmas break to shampoo and curl Santa beards. For spring break, it was the Easter costumes, "bunnies and blood," for mall appearances and church passion plays. Then came the long, dull summer and then Halloween again.

Prologue

Even when I would be otherwise employed at other times of other years, I would often return to Raleigh Creative Costumes for Halloween to help with all the chaos and take in all the excitement. That was the time of year when other former employees showed back up again too, all pitching in together.

Halloween at the shop was my first experience of being truly exhausted at a job, which taught me how good it feels, after working hard and caring about your work, to sit for just a moment and have a bite to eat, especially if that bite is bought for you by your boss as ours sometimes was. We toughed out the stressful times with laughter and with the occasional adult beverages, which were kept in the sewing room. I'd be handling yet another costume fitting, fetching this item and that, pushing through throngs of confused customers who didn't exactly know what they wanted, when a co-worker would inform me of a "meeting" going on in the back and tell me they would finish with this customer for me. The meeting was usually something like a pitcher of margaritas with a few plastic cups beside it, a festive drink to steady us for the seasonal insanity.

The last week of Halloween meant the appearance of "the Ugly Stick," a painted wooden cane with a shrunken head and brass horn attached. Each day as closing time approached, one of us would bring out the Ugly Stick every fifteen minutes of the last hour to announce just how near to closing we were, and never so gleefully as on the night of Halloween itself, a time when the truly desperate would quickly buy from us whatever we had left to offer. A black afro wig and angel wings? Sure. Disco is dead after all. Elvis sunglasses and blue face paint? Why not? We can't rent you the suede shoes though—not unless you could fit into the one Men's size eight we had. And those were the lucky ones. After closing, we chained the front door and any who came after could pound and plead as much as they liked.

My first Halloween, we toasted the end of the madness with shots of Rebel Yell that we drank from Dixie cups—the perfect combination. It tasted awful, but we shared that awfulness together and that made it great.

Halloweens came and went. I graduated college, worked under less surreal conditions, and started looking at heading out of town on a great adventure, which had me thinking about the home I was planning on leaving. I grew up hating our history of prejudices and ignorance, the religious intolerance and bigotry I saw around me.

Prologue

At the same time, I loved my grandmother's cooking, and there was something about the shape of these old streets that just felt right to me, as if my brain had, in its wrinkles and grooves, mimicked the traffic patterns of Five Points, Cameron Village, Fayetteville Street Mall, Hillsborough Street, and Glenwood Avenue.

But it began to dawn on me just how much about my home I did not actually know, how much of my sense of the South and Southern-ness had come through movies and television. And it occurred to me that for almost a decade I had known a woman who understood where I came from better than I did. She had lived a life that witnessed so much transformation in this town, this state, this region, this country, and she had herself gone and left and come back several times, granting her a dual perspective, from within and without, of this, our shared home.

Doug agreed to sit down with me for several Saturdays over the course of a year and related far more than I knew was there to ask. She gave me the gift of her own family legends as well as very personal, very real experiences of her own. Not only did she help me better understand where I come from, she helped a young man just beginning to live his own life to imagine the scope of just how rich a life may be.

Prologue

I present her stories here as she told them, attempting to preserve as much as possible the tone and texture she provided in the telling, as a thanks to her for sharing them and to give all the many people who love her so much and feel so much gratitude toward her an artifact of her life. If you know Miss Doug and you love her, I hope you will find in these pages something of her to treasure.

Part I: Her Words

Chapter One
Making Sherman Pay for Supper

At one time, Warrenton, NC, owned its own railways and its own water and electric systems, independent of the state. I presume sewers went with that, although I know there were an awful lot of privies still there when I was a little girl. They eventually did join with the rest of the world, but the thing that always got my son Joel about Warrenton was that, although it has about a thousand people, which is about what it's always had, it has five hardware stores and probably that many funeral homes. Everybody comes back there to be buried.

The money in Warren County, a lot of it came not only from cotton and tobacco but timber, and still today I would say the main money in town is timber money. That is helped by the government's reforestation programs. You'll see lots of woods there where all the trees are the same size.

Up in this area there are lots of freshwater springs too. There would be a lot of big hotels built there, and people from the plantations—the women and children—in the summer they would go to the springs to "take the waters." There would be dances at night, and this was an opportunity for the young unmarried to meet people from other plantations, so that they would meet those who would be acceptable as mates. This continued on into probably up until the beginning of the 1900s. I used to collect bottles, and I remember when my father's mother saw a Buffalo Springs water bottle in my collection, she said, "Ah, yes, Buffalo Springs—a baby in every bottle," because I'm sure every woman came home pregnant.

My Great-Great-Great Grandmother Temperance, or "Tempy," married John Buxton Williams, who owned five or six hundred acres in Warren County. They first lived in a house called Sunny Hill, which is falling apart now, and then they built Buxton Place. They grew mostly cotton, I would guess, and tobacco and food stuffs. Everything was made down at "The Place," which is still standing and on the historic register.

It's owned by E. B. Harris now, and his family has owned it since the turn of the last century, so there is a graveyard there for his family as well as for the Williamses who are buried there. And once a year, the first Sunday in August, everybody who has any connection with Buxton Place is invited to come and bring a picnic basket. He puts tables out in the grove and brings up baby animals for the city kids to see. And since he's a land auctioneer, he brings speakers and all that, and people tell stories about Buxton Place. You can tour the house and see what restoration he's done since last year.

People have begun to take furniture back there. I had a table that had been made originally as a candle stand on The Place. When I think about all the people, all the family, who are descended from John Buxton and Tempy, and all of us who have their furniture, portraits, quilts, and tableware, it must have been a hell of a lot of stuff they had.

Anyway, John Buxton was in Raleigh when he heard that Joe Johnson had surrendered over at Bennett Place, near Goldsboro. That was after Appomattox. Everybody thinks Appomattox finished the war, but it didn't. And you understand when I talk about "*the* war," it's "The War Between the States," "The Late Unpleasantness," whatever you want to call it, The Civil War. John Buxton knew then that the Union army would be marching north. Raleigh was the first capital they came to in peace. That's the reason the capitol building was not burned. However, they camped there, and the saying is that the weathervane on top of Christ Church was the only chicken in Raleigh when they left. They were living off the land, the way all armies did then.

So John Buxton realized they would be shortly in Warren County, but he knew he could get there quicker riding by himself. He got on his horse and galloped home.

Upstairs at Buxton Place is "The Boys Room," and the floor was taken up in The Boys Room. The meat out of the smoke house was all put down under the floorboards, against the ceiling of the room below, and they put the floor back down and the rug on top. You have to remember, this was probably done by the slaves because that was heavy labor. But there were chickens still there—you couldn't exactly stuff them into the floorboards—and a little bit of meat they couldn't fit.

So Sherman came in with his army. Some of them were over at Cherry Hill plantation nearby, which was built by the same architect as Buxton Place and is practically its mirror image, but the majority of Sherman's army came and camped in the grove at Buxton Place, and Sherman demanded that his troops be fed.

There's a story about The Place in one of the numerous memoirs that were written after the war. This was a woman who was married to one of the members of the Cabinet, and she said that they would go from Richmond to Buxton Place to replenish their food supply. John Buxton had not approved of the secession; he did not believe the South had the resources to fight the North. So when North Carolina seceded, he went out and bought a country store so that he would be supplied during the war. He just bought the whole store and took it home so he would have paint and the things he needed. Buxton Place then would supply cousins, friends, and neighbors. Nobody ever left Buxton Place without something.

So Great-Great-Great Grandmother Tempy said to General Sherman, "I've never turned anybody away from my house hungry, but I do have one request to make."

And Sherman said, "Well, what is that, madam?"

And Tempy said, "I want to speak to your troops." Sherman agreed. They were all mustered in the yard, and she stood on the porch at Buxton Place and said, "You can have all the chickens you see running around, but I want you to go home and tell your wives and your mothers and your sweethearts how you have come south and made war against women and children." Then she fed them.

The officers ate in the house, and after they had eaten and spent the night, she presented Sherman with a bill, and he paid. He paid in "greenbacks," which was what they called US Federal currency, Union money. They say those were the first greenbacks that came into Warren County, and the people around John Buxton borrowed those greenbacks to re-establish connections with their factors in New York, who made the arrangements to sell their cotton in England. Those who didn't have greenbacks, who only had Confederate money, they had nothing.

Land up there wasn't worth anything. Everybody was land-poor. They couldn't afford to work the land because it had all been done with the idea of slave labor, and while they had to support those slaves, that's still cheaper than having to pay each person. There were a certain amount of slaves who didn't want to go back to work as field hands. So they might go north or they might have ended up being a tenant farmer on somebody else's land. But by my generation, and I'm sure my mother's generation, there was still lots of sharecropping at the big houses like Buxton Place and Cherry Hill.

One of the things I do think should be mentioned about the Old South is that slaves did have access to guns. I have a book that has the notes from what we would call city council meetings from before the war. One of the pages in there tells of what the punishment shall be for a white man who fires a gun within the town limits or a white woman who fires a gun within town limits or a free black man or a free black woman or a slave who fires within the town limits. So he had to have a gun to be able to fire it.

I do know that when John Buxton went to Petersburg to get his son Harry's body after the battle of Malvern Hill, he took a slave with him who sat on top of the casket they bought in Petersburg to protect it from people who were trying to steal caskets, because so many people had been killed there, and that slave sat on top of the casket with a gun.

There were two distinct classes of slaves. Most people know this. You had house servants and then you had field hands. The house servants are often the ones who Mulattoes are descended from because they were in the house and they were more accessible to the males in the house. A Mulatto's social status depended on where they were and when. Some of these children of a white man and a slave were sometimes taken into the family.

I was at Cherry Hill one day years ago. There was a man named Austin—the Austins own

Cherry Hill—and one of this current generation of Austins went out looking for other Austins. He found that one of the other Austins, a black Austin, plays oboe for an orchestra in New York. So they made the arrangements some way, and PBS did a film on it. They came out and filmed at Cherry Hill because he did a concert down there. These concerts are done inside Cherry Hill normally, but this particular one was done in the middle of the summer, so they had an outdoor stage. I was on the board of Cherry Hill at the time, and there was a great controversy. How are the people in Warrenton going to take this, with inviting all the slave descendants? How are the blacks going to take this? Will they come? Will they be angry? What are they going to do? Will whites come to the concert?

It was decided that PBS would furnish food out in the grove. They also rented porta potties that they put in the back. Then they had board members stationed all through the house so that during the intermission, when people always wander through the house, there would be somebody to talk to everybody who had any questions in any of the rooms of the house.

So I was working the upstairs, and it was really interesting the things I heard from the blacks who were there. I remember a black woman who brought two little boys with her, and she said, "I want you to see how they lived and what your grandmother was talking about when she talked about 'the fine house.'"

Then I was out in the yard and I heard one man who said, "I never thought I would tread the ground my grandfather tread."

Another man said, "I wish my grandmother had lived to see this day because she always told me about the big white house where she worked."

John Buxton's son Romeo Williams, my great-great uncle, was evidently in love with my great grandmother Eva Douglas Thornton. In the Boys Room you can see Romeo and Eva's names scratched together. But you also see Eva's name scratched with Solomon, and she ended up marrying Solomon.

Romeo then moved in with a black woman. Of course they couldn't legally marry. This was never talked about when I was little. I knew some of it, but it was much later before I learned a lot of this. This would have been after the war, so she was free, but she and all the other former slaves were all still living at Buxton Place. Actually, she was Mulatto. I'm not sure who her father was. I know she was born on the kitchen floor at Buxton Place because I've talked to her great grandson.

Her Words

Every small town has old maid sisters. When Miss Lillybell, the oldest of those in Warrenton died, my cousin Scotty's mother, who was also called "Big Scotty," got a phone call from somebody in New York, a gentleman named Jonas Perry, who said he had just read his copy of *The Warren Record* and seen that Miss Lillybell died, and he just felt like he had to speak to someone in the family to see what had gone on and who else might still be living. So he and Big Scotty talked a while, and he seemed to know all the family stories, but she said they were all told from a little different view, until finally she said, "Mr. Perry, I hope you don't consider this amiss, but are you black?"

And Mr. Perry said, "Yes, my mother was born on the kitchen floor at Buxton Place."

And Scotty said, "Well, I would love to talk to you. If you ever come down south, please come to see me." So he came, and he had pictures of the family members and knew all sorts of ins and outs about other people in the family. He had copies of John Buxton's will. John Buxton left each of his children lots of land, and Romeo deeded a good bit of his portion to a black Baptist church that's still up there called St. Simeon.

One time Jonas and two of his nephews and a niece came down to my lake house, and my cousin

John Henderson came over, and we all spent a day out there together, all of us swapping family pictures. The thing that really got me was that when Jonas saw me, he said, "You look just like the Hintons." My Grandmother Daisy was first cousin of the Hintons who came from Midway plantation. See, all of these plantation people were interrelated because there was nobody else for them to marry.

I said, "Well, I look just like my mother."

And he said, "Well, you look just like all the Hintons."

Before we broke up the afternoon, we were taking pictures. My mother never liked to have her picture made. For some reason, whenever somebody would point a camera at her, she did her mouth up in this strange way, and this woman there did the same thing. And I said, "You don't have to prove anything else to me. You look so much like my mother, it's right spooky."

Anyway, all the stories I heard about Great-Great Uncle Romeo when I was growing up told how he was sort of shiftless. He bought a mule that would balk because he said he had just as much time as the mule. One time, somebody hired him to weigh cotton at the cotton gin, and at the end of the first day, they asked him, "How much cotton did you weigh?"

And he said, "You didn't tell me to write it down. I just weighed it."

But my mother said that he was always very good to my Grandmother Daisy, who would have been his niece. He used to bring stuff from the country for them, and mother said she could remember that when he would travel, if it was a cold day, he would stuff newspapers in his coat to keep warm.

My grandmother Daisy got married very young. She married a man named John Leonard Henderson who was maybe 20 years older. He had been married to her oldest sister, Genell, who was always referred to as just "Nell," and who had died right after they had a child. Genell and John had a baby boy named Archibald, and "Little Baldy" died with jaundice. Then Genell died herself.

When Daisy was a teenage girl, she and her friends were "walking the table." It's something that teenage girls liked to do. If a table has no metal parts, you put your hands on the table and say, "If there is a spirit in the room, will the table please rise?" And this table will move if you have a medium in the group. And they'll always ask, "Who am I going to marry? What's his name?" or "What are his initials?" It will tap one for A, two for B, and so forth. And for Daisy it tapped out, "You will be happier not knowing." In truth she really would have been happier not knowing, because at that time her sister Genell was much in love with John Henderson.

He was a tobacco buyer, and like many people in Warrenton, he didn't think that Duke would ever make any money because Duke was illiterate, so he refused to sign on with him. Many men in Warrenton made this mistake.

Anyway, Grandmother Daisy married John Leonard Henderson, grandson of one of the first three NC Supreme Court justices, and when he went to talk to her father, Grandpa Saul, who my mother always referred to as "Papa," he objected because he thought the family connection was too close. So her sister Sue walked Daisy down the aisle of the Methodist church in Warrenton and gave her away. Don't you know that created talk in town. This was before women even had the vote.

John Leonard Henderson died with pneumonia and left grandmother Daisy with three small children, including my mother, Agnes Hare Henderson. Grandmother Daisy never remarried. I didn't know her. She died when I was only eighteen-months old. But I heard that my mother was much like her. My mother was a very funny person, lots of dry wit, and evidently Grandmother Daisy was too because the story goes that one day she was walking down the street in Warrenton some man was talking to her and said, "Daisy, I hope you go to hell."

And she said, "What a thing to say to me!"

And he said, "Well, I know I'm going to hell and I want somebody there to entertain me."

Chapter Two
Miss Mill Gets to Vote

I was born December 5, 1927, in Durham at Watts hospital, and I was given the name at birth of Douglas Thornton Taylor. Douglas is a family name and wasn't necessarily considered a boy's name at the time. It wasn't until at least 1985 when more Northerners were moving into North Carolina that I really had to start explaining my name. Later on, I found that I could tell which phone call was a telemarketer by how they used my name. They would ask, "Can I speak to Mr. Douglas Haas?"

And I would say, "Oh, he's not here right now."

My father, Joseph White Taylor from Oxford, NC, was one of seven Taylor sons, but I was not the seventh son of a seventh son. I was an only child. And as I said, my mother was Agnes Hare Henderson. Incidentally, Haas is the German form of "Hare," which I think is sort of an interesting little side note since I would later marry a Haas.

Both my parents came from early settlers in North Carolina whose family had moved down from Virginia, and, you know, North Carolina really had no input of new people coming into the coastal area until the Montagnards came in. The Montagnards were the Vietnamese mountain people who fought alongside the Americans against the Viet Cong and then were given refuge here after the Vietnam War. Many of them came to North Carolina, I presume because of the military bases, because they would be sponsored by some soldier they had known.

The Piedmont had its immigration with the Moravians and Scots-Irish coming there, but the coastal plains hadn't had any new people coming in much after the 1600s. Anybody who was here pretty much stayed here and intermarried, so all of these are family names that go way back in North Carolina, South Carolina, and Virginia, but particularly in North Carolina in that area.

My parents were fifth cousins. In fact, one of my father's brothers was named for my mother's great grandfather. Trying to sort out eastern North Carolina's family connections takes a Philadelphia lawyer.

My father was tall, another one of "those long-legged Taylors." And my mother had been so tiny that my father said he wouldn't marry her until she weighed a hundred pounds.

She was the first girl in town to walk in a barber shop and have her hair bobbed. And I mean, that was quite a big deal. It wasn't just that she had her hair bobbed, but ladies did not even look in the window as they passed by a barbershop then. And in the South, most barbers were black. My uncle, who moved to Philadelphia, had told me how embarrassed he was for the first white barber who ever cut his hair. So she had a little Dutch boy cut.

Anyway, he finally married her when she weighed 98. He didn't wait any longer.

When they celebrated their fiftieth wedding anniversary, somebody asked him about how he always referred to her as "my pretty old lady," and my mother said, "But I've gained so much weight."

And he said, "Well, it wasn't but two pounds a year, and that's hardly noticeable." He was a diplomat.

He wore a fedora on the back of his head, as all engineers then were prone to do as they got older, although in the picture I have of him on his first job, he's wearing a sort of cap. At that time the engineering school was located at the University of North Carolina at Chapel Hill. When he and his roommate were in Chapel Hill, they lived in Old

East, and they had one of the two cars on campus owned by students, but they had built theirs. They were both engineering students, and so they built the engine and all of that, and then they took it to a wagon maker and had him build the body. I've always been so disappointed there were never any pictures of it. He graduated in 1922 and said he was the only person in that class who didn't claim to have roomed with Thomas Wolfe, who also graduated in '22.

My father had absolutely the most beautiful handwriting you can imagine. When he graduated, they kept his notebooks to use as examples for future students as to how to keep notes. His handwriting was also the reason he was the last to be discharged from his US officer training unit after the First World War. All the men there, as they turned 18, were immediately inducted into the military in an officer program, so I have one picture of him in a uniform, holding a gun. He was a really good shot, having grown up in the country. In fact, I have a picture of him while he was still in dresses—you know they kept little boys in dresses then—holding onto two guns, there with his dog.

Anyway, he said that he was issued a gun one day, and he went home and cleaned it. The next day was the Armistice. So the only thing he did in the military was he cleaned all the cosmoline out of that gun. But he was the last person who was released because they kept him there to write all of the official papers to issue the discharges. He was in there less than three months, so he was never eligible for any veteran's benefits. I remember when he died, it was after my first husband Ben died, and I knew from that experience that the Veterans Administration would furnish us a stone, but my father had told me he wasn't in long enough.

He was very precise. His friends would laugh and say he probably could use a slide rule to tell time because he could do anything with a slide rule. You know, engineers at that time were known for wearing a slide rule on their belts. So he taught me to check my multiplication and division by slide rule when I was in fourth grade.

I really wanted to be an engineer, and my father never discouraged me. When I was little, he would take me to work. I liked to watch the steam shovels. He wouldn't ever let me get on one though. I was disappointed in that. He wouldn't let me ride a motorcycle with one of the highway patrolmen who worked out at his office either. I was disappointed in that also. He was somewhat protective, but at the same time, if I wanted to, I could go out and watch them build a road and listen to them talk about it. At that time, it was during the Depression, and state employees could eat at the prisons, so I remember eating at the prisons with the guards and the staff. They always had a prisoner assigned to stand right behind me and get me whatever I wanted. I lived a very indulged childhood, I realize now.

When the war started in 1860, Lee decided to go with the state instead of the nation. He was offered the command of the American armies and said, no, he would go with his state. So he sent his wife and children to Jones Springs in Warren County. I can remember being out there and seeing the falling-down building. My mother wouldn't let me go with the little boys who went and explored it. She was afraid I would fall through the floor.

There is a marker there because one of the girls, Annie Carter Lee, died from typhoid fever there, and so she's buried in the Jones cemetery. The black population around there took it on as a project. They didn't like the idea of there being a historic marker there marking the place of the burial of Lee's daughter, and so they kept knocking the marker down.

I was there as a child with my father the day they put the marker up. The women of the United Daughters of the Confederacy (UDC) had campaigned to get this marker put there, and so they had called my father and said, "Can you get a man to come and put it up?"

There was a black prison up there, and they built the highways at that time with prison labor, so my father was familiar with hiring black prisoners. He went by that prison and picked up the strongest black man he saw, and I can remember Miss Ammer Graham wringing her hands when she saw them. "Oh, Mr. Taylor! I thought you would bring somebody else!"

My father said later, "I wonder who she thought was going to put it up? Did she think I was bringing the governor?"

All the other Lee family is buried at Washington and Lee University up in Virginia, and they wanted Annie Carter to be moved there too. Of course, by this time, a hundred years later, there was nothing there of Annie but dirt, so they took a bucket of dirt, and there was one brass handle that they found from the coffin. That is what is interred now at Washington and Lee. The historic marker is still up on the road in Warrenton. It was never taken down again since, technically, she ain't there.

My mother would today be considered a paralegal. She was reading law when my parents were married and keeping books at a furniture store and teaching typing too, I think, and shorthand. My father said she had five jobs. She then would work off and on during the Depression as a court stenographer, and sometimes would also work in Jules Banzet's office. He was a lawyer who later became a judge in Warrenton. During the Second World War when we lived in Raleigh, she worked for North Carolina military and was the stenographer that did all the secret typings and whatnot. She also took depositions for the Nuremberg trials from people who had to be interviewed here.

Most of the women for several generations in my family were expected to be educated. They were very forward-thinking. I noticed that I have a lot of friends who their mother or themselves are really the first generation of women in their family that were expected to finish high school or certainly to have any further education. In fact, the idea was early on that I would grow up to be a professional woman and should use just the name "Douglas Thornton" instead of taking a husband's name, and frankly, that's what I should have done. Then I wouldn't have had the confusion of being Haas or Bennet.

My father's one sister graduated from St. Mary's Junior College in Raleigh and later taught school. She wanted to be a nurse, but her family didn't think that was a proper thing for a Southern lady to do. You might see a nude man. Of course, she'd grown up with seven brothers. She had to have known everything that any man had. Finally, she became a volunteer nurse's aide during the war. She came and lived with us and worked at Rex Hospital. She and my mother both worked as nurse's aides at Rex during the war. But Miss Mary—I called her "Mamie," but a lot of the family called her Miss Mary—worked I think more hours than any other aide they had and ended up with lots of specialized training. So after the war, she ended up with a paid permanent job as a nurse's aide at the military hospital in Columbia, SC, at Fort Jackson in the maternity ward.

Mamie was a wiry little woman. One time my son John was sitting on her lap and he said, "Mamie, you'd be good for me to use to study anatomy, because I can feel all your bones." They tell the story of one Thanksgiving she said she'd have "the parson's nose" from the turkey, and when they cut it off to serve her, she said, "Oh, only half of it!"

I had one great aunt, Hettie, who had gotten married and moved on to Philadelphia, and, when her husband died, she started a secretarial service, and another great aunt, Alice, who became a concert pianist. She graduated from, the Women's College of Greensboro, which we just called WC, and went to New York for more advanced study. Of course she didn't go alone. It wouldn't have been quite "fittin'." Her sister went along with her. I guess she went in her late teens. She then became an accompanist coach, so her sister Sue went with her and got a job on Wall Street, where almost no women worked at the time. She was working in the office, mostly secretarial work, but she would have been considered a paralegal like my mother. So I come from a family of women who went out and did things like that.

I always called my father "Joe." My mother thought I should say "Father," but he said he was too young to be called "Father." When I was born, he must have been about 28. I would sometimes when I was little simply call him, "my father," but I never shortened it to "Father." I just shortened it to "Joe" because that's what everybody else said, and he liked it. I was of course required to call all of my friends' parents "Mr." and "Mrs.," and I never called my mother anything but "Mother."

I remember when somebody said to my father, "Well, Joe, how do you feel about your daughter calling you 'Joe'?"

And my mother said, "Why should he object? He calls his own mother 'Miss.'"

Everyone called my Grandmother Taylor "Miss Mill." She was Mildred Kenon Taylor, and she married George Thomas Taylor, so she was a Taylor before she was married.

After the armistice was signed out at Bennett place, and the Union armies were going north, valuables were buried. Miss Mill was a baby then, and her older sister Lucy heard they were talking about burying all the valuables. She thought the most valuable thing in the house was the new baby, so she took her little baby-sister Mildred, my grandmother, and hid her in the dirty clothes in the wash house.

Miss Mill grew up in a house in Franklin County that was, as some of the architecture people tell me, what is considered the sort of Cadillac of the Jacob Holt houses. Jacob Holt was a famous builder in eastern North Carolina and Virginia. I was taken there once when I was a child and saw the chair rails that had little roses that had been carved in them, and Miss Mill told me that the slaves had carved those.

The stairwell is painted in such a way, it looks as if the stairwell is made out of marble, big blocks of marble. It's wood of course. A lot of the houses in Warren County and all that area that Jacob

Holt—or his disciple Mr. Waddell—built have marbleized baseboards or other wooden features that have been painted to represent finer woods instead of the pine with which they were all built.

When I would be at my grandmother's in Oxford, the cook, who was black, would bring her little girl, Dorothy, and we would play together. Dorothy didn't come into the dining room to eat. She might eat in the kitchen, and sometimes she and I would eat a snack on the back steps together or we would go down in the garden. She showed me how to get a cantaloupe out of the garden and break it on a tree and stick your face in it, and very frankly there is no cantaloupe as good as that.

There was also a man named Otis who lived at my grandmother's. I don't remember what he did on the farm, but I do know that if my grandmother wanted to go somewhere, he'd put on his jacket and his chauffeur's cap and drive this big long Buick, and she would go to town. It wasn't that far between Oxford and Warrenton, and if they'd be passing by, I could ride back and forth. So I stayed with my grandmother in Oxford a lot. When I would go downtown with her, she would do her shopping and usually give me a nickel at Hall's drugstore to get ice cream.

One time though, there was an election. This is something that has always stuck with me. I don't know why Otis was not available to take her to vote, but I know that somebody hooked up the buggy and that she took me with her. Evidently there had been some controversy about her going to vote, so nobody had time to take her. See, the right for women to vote hadn't come in until the '20s, so I was probably six or seven years old.

We went down the roads, which were most of them dirt, and she drove me to the voting precinct, which was over in some little town near Oxford but not in Oxford. I can remember how she sat very straight driving, and she had her little gloves on. We went to this little country store where she voted, and we got back in the little buggy and she went home.

It was hard to tell a person's social class then, during the Depression. Some people had jobs and some people didn't. My father said that at the time some of the best roads were done in North Carolina because he didn't have a truck driver working for him who didn't have an engineering degree.

My uncle John sold insurance. He lived with us. We lived in the house my grandfather had built my grandmother before they were married that she never went into until after they were married, because it wouldn't have been considered "fittin'." So uncle John lived there with my parents, and so I just assumed he was my third parent. The house is still there in Warrenton, behind the post office.

Nobody was buying insurance. Nobody could afford it. His friend sold automobiles, and no one was buying those. So they weren't paying any rent. Mother rented a room to two school teachers. Then, during tobacco season—because, at that time, there were tobacco markets right across the street from us—the tobacco buyers would come over to our house and pay to eat. My father's salary had been cut back—not "cut." The state of North Carolina said that they "borrowed" from their employees' salary, but it was never paid back. He was making, I think, $100 a month, but at the same time, we had a cook, we had a yard man, and we had a laundrist; and this was not unusual. They lived next door.

My parents were not wealthy. We inherited stuff but no money. You know, there is a Southern saying, "We were so poor, we had to drink out of the silver goblets." They weren't bragging. It was a statement of fact, that this part of North Carolina was very rich before the war.

We were considered "old family." We were old plantation stock. There was just no money, and eventually, down to my generation, nobody could afford to get new furniture, so we were all living with antiques that we couldn't have afforded. They were considered "Mother's Attic" then.

I have the tea part of a silver service, a beautiful tankard and a butter dish. It's a round, silver dish, and in the bottom part there is a glass piece that separates the two parts of this globe. The glass part has been incised with a design of a little kid that you could press down on the butter so you could make it look nice. Then you filled the bottom part with ice to keep the butter from melting when you put it on the table. There was also a little hook where you put the butter knife. When Aunt Lucy hid Miss Mill in the laundry, these were all buried in the yard.

Chapter Three
It Isn't Always Going to Be Like This

We moved from Warrenton to Raleigh when I was ten years old. In Raleigh there were fewer racial tensions than Warrenton. There of course was St. Augustine's and Shaw University, so there was a whole class of educated blacks. Oberlin Road had beautiful homes on it, as nice as anything you would see of the white homes on Saint Mary's Street, which runs parallel to it, and those belonged to black doctors and lawyers. There are some that are still there. The Turners and the Rochelles are still there. The Turners still own that big house of theirs. In fact, there was a story, I think, in *The News and Observer* about their family. It showed pictures of them and the inside of that house is furnished beautifully with antiques like any Old Raleigh place would have.

The Wilson Temple Methodist Church there on Oberlin is as much involved with good works in Raleigh as any white Methodist church in town. There are times when my church, West Raleigh Presbyterian, has worked with them in tutoring

English as a second language and things like that. They are involved with the prison ministry too. There are several black churches that are very involved in the prison ministry.

One of the interesting things about that church is Edenton Street Methodist, a white church, had a big fire in the '30s or '40s, and the brick masons and other builders—because most of the skilled labor were black; there were doctors and lawyers too, but if you wanted a skilled brick mason, you usually got a black person—they went down and donated labor to work on Edenton Street Methodist Church. So when Wilson had a big fire and a good bit of it burned too, Edenton Street came and returned the favor.

Certainly still the schools were segregated. I can't remember how soon the Oberlin School was closed and the children from Oberlin came to Fred Olds, but that worked very well. There was no real problem, primarily because these children at that time had a cultural similarity. They said, "Yes, ma'am," and, "Yes, sir," and frankly we played together as children. We used to play down in the woods where Cameron Village is now. We did not go into each other's homes, but we played together outside.

I would grow up to work in costumes, and I did sew when I was little. I was around women who sewed. Miss Mill sewed beautifully. I have a quilt that she made that I hang up on my wall. Aunt Lucy would come and visit us, and she would sew. Between the two of them, they would make our clothes. My mother's mother sewed beautifully too, but Mother did not, and so when I got to be a teenager—it was during the Depression and I wanted more clothes—I started teaching myself to sew.

And Maggie, who worked for us in Raleigh, also sewed beautifully, and she helped me learn how to sew. She also told me that things weren't always going to be like this. I remember one day when I was a teenager, she was ironing my father's shirts, and she said, "You better let me teach you how to iron these shirts. A little boy is going to want you to iron his shirts one day. You know it's not always going to be like this." And I must say she was right, because I've ironed a hell of a lot of shirts for little boys, back before there were drip-dry fabrics.

Maggie was an interesting dichotomy for the South too. It was Maggie's story that actually got Simon & Schuster to give my first husband Ben an advance to write his novel *Look Away, Look Away*. They told him that they thought the question of Civil Rights was going to be over in a couple of years, and so Ben should hurry and write this because it would be a dead issue. This was in the late '50s. He explained to them that the South was an entirely different area from what they knew. "The editor from one of your major newspapers is the uncle of the woman who helped raise my wife," he said, "and I'm sure he would never publicize this in New York City, but when he comes to Raleigh and stays at the Sir Walter Hotel and the family gathers there, she is invited too." That was Maggie.

She was one of the Roysters. Vermont Connecticut Royster was editor of *The Wall Street Journal* and he retired to *The News and Observer*, the Raleigh newspaper. His father had said he was tired of all the children being called, "That's Mary's Tom," or, "That's Tom's Mary," or, "That's Betty's Mary," or, "That's Betty's Tom." And he said, "My children are all going to have their own names," so he named them all after the states. There's still Roysters here in Raleigh having these names. The story is the only one whose name came out okay was one of the daughters who was named Virginia Carolina.

Maggie's father was Alabama Arkansas. Her mother, who I think was one of the Boylans, was, you know, mulatto from one of the Boylans. I always called her "Miss Minnie." So the editor of *The News and Observer* was my maid's uncle, although by the time he became editor of the paper, Maggie had died.

So the relationships were a lot more complicated than others might think. All whites were not out to lynch all blacks. At that time very much there was a feeling that all Southerners were rednecks, all Klansmen—although there used to be a sign in Johnston County that had a picture of a knight rider, saying, "We are against Integration and Communism," and both of them were misspelled but I can't recall how.

But there was a whole other set of people. It may be politically incorrect to say this, but it was the plantation people. I think liberality is connected with a more educated segment. People forget that there was a great respect for education among the planter class, that the University of North Carolina at Chapel Hill was the first state-supported university in the United States. And the women in my ancestry were all either tutored at home with the boys or sent to school. The women's colleges of North Carolina, St. Mary's and Peace, both of those schools were in existence before the Civil War. The Graham School over at Chapel Hill, with Frank Porter Graham—well, the Grahams have been into education and had schools in North Carolina since the early 1800s that I know of, because we lived next to a Graham school that was a boarding school for boys but also took girls that lived in town. That closed when the state opened public high schools. The Jewish family Mordecai also had a girl's school in Warrenton, before they moved the school to Raleigh and joined Christ Church.

My great-grandmother Eva Douglas Thornton met my great-grandfather Solomon Buxton Williams when she came to the Warrenton Female Academy to go to school. She must have been about twelve or thirteen. That building is still standing. I don't even think it has a historic marker there saying this was a girl's school at that time.

Now, when I say this, I don't mean that everybody who was part of the educated Old South was for integration. It kind of depended a great deal on what their experiences had been. And they were against integration in a different way from the way the rednecks would be against integration.

But the classes under them, usually the overseers on a plantation, were more likely to be anti-black. The same went for the carpetbaggers who came down from the North. Maggie used to go in the summer and work up in Baltimore, and she would make a lot more money than she would make here, so my mother said, "Maggie, why don't you stay in Baltimore? Why do you come back?"

And she said, "When I'm in Baltimore, it's too segregated. I never know what store I can go in and what store I can't." And Maggie was just as white as me. She would travel with my mother sometimes and they would eat in nice restaurants that said, "We don't serve blacks." She was "passing."

Maggie's son, Christopher Grey, had also been "passing," and he enlisted in the Navy before the First World War, but Maggie didn't want him fighting. At that time the only way a black could serve in the Navy was as a cook, so she went and declared him black. He survived the war and later became dean of Shaw University.

I would say that my parents, for the times, were thought very liberal. Nowadays they would have been considered sort of paternalistic, but at the same time, as soon as it was possible for Social Security to be paid on domestic help, my father immediately made sure that our domestic help was listed and paid Social Security on them. Taking care of people is in many ways a really liberal thing to do. I know that we had people working for us during the Depression, and there wasn't that much money around. I'm sure my parents still felt responsible for them though, because they had to eat and take care of their children. I well-remember being told when I outgrew my tricycle that Santa Claus was going to pick it up and take it to the black family down the street for their little girl for Christmas.

And that just seemed the thing that was going to happen, even though I very much wanted a scooter. I had been told that this was a very hard Christmas and Santa Claus might not be able to afford a scooter, that maybe I might get something else. It would be something nice. What I really wanted was a scooter.

Well, Christmas morning there was a bright orange scooter under the tree for me. It seems that my uncle John and his friend Jimmy Mayfield, who also lived at our house and didn't pay any rent because he didn't have a job, somewhere out in the country, they had found a scooter that was rusty. They took it and sanded it, and at that time all state highway equipment was painted bright orange. I have a feeling this scooter was painted with "liberated" paint. So I got a scooter.

My father was not hesitant to use the "N-word." That was just what black people were called, but at the same time someone asked him once how he addressed the principle over at O'Kelly School, a black school, when he had to go in and see which roads had to be cleared. They said, "How do you deal with him? How do you speak to him?"

And my father said, "Well, I call him 'doctor.' He's got more education than I have."

Ladies didn't use the "N-word." We used the term "colored people." I still occasionally use that because it's so natural. I remember going to visit my uncle and aunt in Philadelphia when I was eighteen. My Aunt Belle was from Warrenton, VA, but she would have been a really staunch abolitionist. Now one thing ladies did do was we might say "negro," so she was very particular that I would get enough "e" in that word. Well my mother wasn't real fond of Belle anyway. Belle really tore it with my mother when she called and said she was so pleased that I was so polite to her black help. Mother hit the ceiling because of course I'd always been taught to be considerate of people who were working for us.

And I think that held true throughout a good bit of the South. I can't speak to the very deep South, but I know that one of the things that Ben and I found when we had been doing some research down in Atlanta once was that some of the first protests against lynchings in the South were staged by educated white women. What they did was, when it came to the point that a black man would be tried for what they felt was an unjust thing and he was going to be railroaded, they would go to court and just sit quietly in court and then go home and report to their husbands on what was being said and make sure that their husbands took pains to do something about this. Perhaps they withheld themselves; there were just all sorts of ways.

It was the planters who had been raised to look after their people. After all, you know, it's sort of foolish to work a horse to death. That's something that I think is very seldom noted. Yes, there were people who were not good slaveholders just as there are those who were not good employers. There were people like the people who hired those girls who worked in that shirt factory in New York that burned.

As a way of trying to explain to my children how their grandparents viewed black people in a different light, I used to read them—because I read aloud to kids a lot—the "Miss Minerva" stories. They were a series of books. *Miss Minerva and William Green Hill*, that was the title of the first one. Miss Minerva was white. She was William Green Hill's aunt, and after his parents died, he had been taken care of by his Uncle Jimmy-Jawed Jupiter. But he had a little black playmate named Wilkes Booth Lincoln who is brought to town to live with them by the Major, a Civil War veteran who Miss Minerva marries.

In the second book, *Billy and the Major*, William Green Hill is going off to school, and the Major says he will see to it that Wilkes Booth Lincoln gets to go as well. When Miss Minerva reacts in surprise, the Major says, "Certainly I should be ashamed to look my Maker in the face if I did not try to let him get as good an education as our nephew."

The books were so popular that even though the author Francis Boyd Calhoun, who lived in Warrenton incidentally, died, they hired other writers to keep writing Miss Minerva stories. But the stories about the interactions between little boys and little girls and their black neighbors and black maids and nurses are very much a story of the sort of time my parents grew up in. My mother told me that some of the stories she knew actually happened in Warrenton.

In Raleigh, I met my friend Wat. She and I both entered Needham Broughton High School as what were called "sub-freshman." At that time they had four years of high school and this one year of sub-freshman over there. It hadn't been too many years since the state of North Carolina had voted to require twelve years for high school. I remember my father voting against it because he said he didn't think that they would enhance what they were teaching so much as take longer to teach the same thing. History did seem to show that to be the case as I went through high school there at Broughton and later there as my children went through.

I had been in grammar school at Fred Olds, and Wat had been in grammar school at Ravenscroft, a private school. Ravenscroft at that time didn't go any farther than sixth grade, so she transferred to Broughton. We ended up being in the same home room because at that time the homerooms were divided up alphabetically, and T and W ended up being in the same room. She was Mary Frances Watson. That's the reason she was called "Wat." There was at that time a little symbol for electricity to promote using more electricity in the home, and it was this little sketch of something called Kilowatt. I don't remember exactly when she started being known as Wat, probably as we got old enough to date, and she'd be kidding that she was a Kilowatt. So it became Wat, and for those of us who have known her always, it's always Wat.

She would take music lessons somewhere up near Five Points. By that time my parents had moved up onto Sunset Avenue, which is right behind the big Baptist church up there. And so, when we were having supper, Wat would come in and she would say, "Oh, Miz Taylor! Can I have just a little taste of that?" And Mother would give her a bread and butter plate with a little taste on it. And Wat would say, "Can I have a little taste of that too?" My mother used to say that Wat was the only person she ever saw who could eat a five-course meal on a plate for bread and butter.

But we did become good friends. We were very tightly knit. Wat was a very attractive-looking redhead, a real strawberry blonde with very pale skin and a good figure. She was not athletic. I was not into sports either, but I did like to swim. I worked at camps and would work on the waterfront some. Because of how she was so sensitive to the sun, Wat wouldn't even do those sort of sports, but she was always a sports fanatic, watching it. She loved to go to ball games and later, when she couldn't get out as much, she would love to watch any sort of sport on TV— basketball, football, soccer—particularly if Carolina was playing. I don't care who Carolina was playing, she was there, rooting for them. Well, of course she had graduated from Carolina with a degree in English before going up to New York to the American Academy for acting. And Wat danced. I'm sure she danced as part of her theater training, and sang, also as part of her theater training.

When I first met Wat, I don't remember having a great deal of interest in theater myself. I had a few other friends who were not theater oriented, but we did go to the movies. The movie reels changed two or three times a week downtown. At that time, you could go and walk in the movie at any time and stay until you saw the movie through to where you came in, since they just ran a continuous strip.

We would go to either the Ambassador or the State movie theaters. There was also the Palace. They showed cowboy movies, and little boys would go there. The Wake on Fayetteville Street was sort of iffy. Sometimes they showed movies that we would go to and sometimes not. But we seldom missed anything that was being shown at the Ambassador, maybe a little more seldom than what was being shown at the State, although I do remember going to travelling theater performances at the State. All these movie theaters are now closed.

The Lincoln movie theater was a movie theater that catered just to the black community. The other movie theaters all had side entrances for blacks to go through and a balcony above the balcony where whites sat. It's interesting that the

Lincoln Theater is the one that survives, and it now operates as a music venue.

The Rialto was built just before the Second World War. It was the first suburban theater and it was called the Colony, which for people my age at times has been confusing. When I came back to Raleigh in the '70s, the Colony had become the Rialto and another theater named the Colony opened up. Somebody would say to go to the Colony, and I would meet them at the Rialto. When it opened, it didn't have the fancy decor that the State had or that the Ambassador had. The State was built with the statuary and the boxes and all that. It was quite lovely.

Gone with the Wind had its first showing in Raleigh at the State. It was a big thing, and my parents invited their best friends over from Warrenton to attend. Their daughter and I were both about ten or eleven years old, but we were allowed to go see it because it was assumed we were "clothed in the eyes of innocence" and didn't recognize what might be going on when Rhett took Scarlet up the stairs. And we didn't know. We really were clothed in the eyes of innocence because I read the book when I was in fifth grade and missed it all. It was a much more innocent time because there were not the TV shows and movies and magazines that had so much sex in them, so we really did not have a lot of knowledge about it.

Wat had been going to camp up at Montreat every summer, and I went to the Girl Scout camp in Raleigh for a month every summer. It was out at what is now Umstead Park. But Wat went up to Montreat to camp, and she had a friend up there named Grace Gordon and they always shared a cabin. Grace lived in Asheville, still does, and her folks had taken her out of school up there and put her in the high school department at Brevard College. Brevard was a Methodist school and considered actually the little sister of Duke at the time, when Duke had closer ties to the Methodist church. The Watsons decided that was a good place for Wat too.

We were having so much upheaval at Broughton High School with teachers coming and going. There had been five chemistry teachers in my last year at Broughton, and my parents said, "You're never going to learn anything in this sort of school environment." The male chemistry teacher would be drafted. The female chemistry teacher would leave to follow her boyfriend or get married. And so it was just a constant change. The Spanish teacher was really a French teacher who had never taken Spanish and was only a page or two ahead of us in the book. The English teacher

I had was really not a strong teacher at all. In fact, she had been a classmate of my mother's at The Women's College in Greensboro, and so when I complained about her, my mother sort of nodded and said, "Yeah, she was just like that in college," a sort of boring person.

There was some talk about different schools that I might be sent to. St. Margaret's was in Richmond. It was an Episcopal girl's school that some of the girls here went to, and it was rather expensive, but I had a great uncle who was there on the board. He said that if I wanted to come, he would see that I went. But I didn't like the idea of going to a girl's school and wearing uniforms, which they had to do. I must have been fifteen or sixteen. Mrs. Dunn, which was up over by Boylan Pearce when Boylan Pearce was downtown, sold the uniforms, and they were little shirtwaist dresses that came in different colors. I was not impressed.

Luckily my parents were rather liberal in their allowing me to make decisions. They must have spoken with the Watsons about Brevard and done some other investigations. So they decided to send me to Brevard with Wat.

Brevard had worked out a thing where they hired retired teachers. It's up in the mountains in a very beautiful place, and that area had become a very popular place to retire. So they offered teachers who were well-known in their field certain perks for coming back to work and coming there.

The English teacher there had rheumatoid arthritis. They offered her a classroom down the hall from where she had a bedroom and private bath and they would bring her meals in. There was a man named Bramlet. I don't know quite what his problem was, but he was quite well-known in the field of economics, and his hands would turn in a funny way. When he was writing on the blackboard in the classroom, there was a certain special little platform that had been built so he could write and reach the blackboard with its help. The blackboard had been tilted just right for him to write on. And he was a wonderful teacher. His wife taught math there. Then there was a woman who taught biology. I never had her, but her husband was in the tuberculosis hospital in Asheville, and so they offered her a place to stay near the hospital if she would come down and teach. She was supposed to be a world-renowned biologist, studying bugs, and the mountains of North Carolina—I found this out—are one of the richest places in the world for bug life.

These teachers were not likely to be drafted. In fact, many of them could not have gotten a job somewhere else. And they were people who are not just your ordinary teacher at any high school. Even if Broughton had teachers that were stable at that time, Brevard had teachers that were a cut above that lot.

They also had Dr. Coltrane at the head of it, and he had a very innovative idea for the time. He divided the year into three parts—the entire year, not just the school year—and in each one of these thirds, as a high school student, you took two complete years of some subject, and then possibly a half a year of some other subject or a subject that didn't give you a full credit. For high school graduation I took art, I remember. At that time a lot of young men were trying to finish high school in a hurry. They could get six or maybe seven credits for going for a year, and at that time you didn't need but maybe fourteen to graduate. He kept that going even after the war for a number of years. I don't know for how many, because I was long out of there, but the vets who had dropped out of high school kept coming back, because they could quickly get through school.

I went along with about twenty other girls and boys from Raleigh to Mars Hill for summer school. I had gotten too old for camp. There wasn't much going on to do. It was during the war. I went up on the train on a sleeper, and the next morning, as we came into the Asheville train station, little news boys were running along the side of the train, screaming, "Extra! Extra!" just like you see it in the old-fashioned movies, and the headlines were the invasion of Europe. So that was June 1944. That was when we went into Omaha beach.

Wat was already there, and her story was that Dean Stephenson stopped her on campus and said, "Mary Frances, we have a new student coming in next semester from Raleigh named Douglas Taylor, and I thought I'd put him over in Ross Hall with Stockton."

And Wat said, "Dean Stephenson, I think you better call her parents about this. Douglas is a girl." It is because of me that there is now a box to check on their school applications for the sex of the applicant.

She and I went to Brevard together and we stayed friends for the rest of her life. She went up to school in New York to the American Academy for acting and then toured in travelling theater productions. The first thing they made her do at the American Academy up there was to lose her Southern accent, and the first professional job shot got was playing a Southern character, so she had to pick it back up.

Chapter Four
This Friend You Ought to Marry

Now Ben's father, Otto Haas, Sr., was a German and had come over as a thirteen-year-old boy, all by himself. One of Otto's older brothers had left Germany and gone to Tennessee, where he had been very successful showing movies--of course these were the early 1900s, the silent films--but when he died, he did not have a child of his own to leave his business, and so little Otto came over and inherited the Tennessee movie theaters from his older brother. I don't know why he eventually came to Charlotte, NC, but he set up several movie theaters there and really became the person who organized the North Carolina Movie Theater Association.

He married Laura Jo Michaels. She was his cashier, and he had a little silver pistol made for her that would fit in her purse because she would carry the receipts home with her. The pistol was so small that the bullets had to be specially made. I can remember Ben and his brother showing me the molds. And she was still a dead shot right up into her late seventies. You didn't mess with her. She was a tiny little thing with a little knot of white hair on top of her head. It looked like she had posed for Disney for the fairy godmother from *Cinderella*. We called her "Shorty."

My family was never wealthy in the way his family had been. They'd had a big house in Dilworth that Shorty had designed. Dilworth was *the* place to live in Charlotte at the time. But Otto made some bad loans during the Great Depression and they had to sell it and move to the country.

Otto was doing some real estate, and he bought this place out there on the edge of Charlotte, this old farmhouse, figuring that the city would move that way, which was very smart. He immediately dug a swimming pool for them out there, and this was in the 1930s, long before it was common. He moved in the crystal chandeliers there that he'd brought from Germany, and he added a bathroom to the house and indoor plumbing. He'd evidently run out of money after that, but he still owned several movie theaters and so he took the swinging doors from one of them and hung those for the bathroom doors. They were at the end of the hall, and as you walked in the house, you would see them swinging.

This Friend You Ought to Marry

Ben said the thing that he remembered about it was not that they didn't live as well as they had. They still had servants but, for the first time, he didn't have a nursemaid, and he thought it was wonderful to have that freedom there. That was very popular then, having a nurse. Until you went to school, you would be very likely to have a nursemaid.

A lot of people finished high school at sixteen in the '40s, and so you weren't drafted until you were eighteen. Ben had gotten the Pepsi Cola scholarship to attend Chapel Hill. At that time, that was like getting a Morehead in that it paid all your expenses for four years, but when Ben was sixteen, his father died. Ben realized that his mother could not get along and take care of herself and his younger brother. His older brother, Otto Haas, Jr., had joined the merchant marines earlier. Later he went into the army, but at that time he was sailing on merchant ships. So Ben quit school, went home, and got a job proofreading at the newspaper.

He was drafted and became a driver for a tank battalion that was to be part of the invasion of Japan, had that been necessary. He ended up in the Philippines and served out the rest of the war there. Many years later, when Ben and I were married, there was a Japanese man who was teaching at North Carolina State University and had his family living here in Raleigh. They were Presbyterians and went to West Raleigh church also. One Sunday afternoon, he and Ben found themselves being the pair of people who were going around together, making calls on the congregation to talk to them about their pledge, and this Japanese man was part of the home guard who was to be standing on the beach, repelling the Americans. So they could have met as enemies instead of out doing their church business.

Most of the people that I dated were in the military or had been in the military, but from the time you were sixteen as a girl you could go to USO dances. I don't know who arranged those, but they wanted to make sure they didn't get any of Katie May's girls. Katie May had a whorehouse here. Back before the Glenwood Avenue bridge was so high over Crabtree Creek, the road came way down and then you turned up to the right and there it was. I remember my father took me by one time and told me not to go to any parties there.

I had a good friend here in Raleigh who lived over in one of those stone houses on the corner of Clark and Shepherd Street. She was Anna Slack, and she was an only child like me. We had met when we entered into Broughton High School.

This Friend You Ought to Marry

Anna had a lot of cousins who came to NC State University, and at one time or another I dated most of them. One of them I dated for a long, long time. Everybody always thought Howard and I would get married. Obviously, we didn't.

Anna went to Chapel Hill as a pharmacy major because at that time, as a female, you couldn't enter Chapel Hill to study as a freshman unless you were going to be a pharmacy major, and she met Ben's best friend, Jim Henderson. Back in the woods outside Charlotte when they were growing up, Ben and Jim used to run a trapline with number one or number two jumps—that means the size of the claws that you put down below the waterline so the animal doesn't struggle and suffer but is immediately drowned. They would go out and bring the animals home and skin them on the dining room table and then sell them. I think mink even then brought about $50 a skin, so it was worth it. That was a lot of money, a lot more than you were making running a paper route or mowing lawns. And Otto, Jr. used to trap with them. He trapped enough mink for his wife to have a mink stole.

Both Ben and Jim had just gotten out of the military. So one day we were sitting in the breakfast room over at Anna's family's house, and

Jim said, "You know, Doug, I've got this friend you ought to marry."

And I said, "Well, I haven't met him, Jim." I was at a college in Richmond, and I had come down to date this guy—whose name also was Doug, oddly enough. I can't remember his last name.

The next time Ben and I were both visiting in town at the same time, Doug had invited me down to this weekend of parties and dances, the black and white formals. The tea dances were afternoon dances, and then there was another dance that night.

Anyway, Anna called and said, "Jim brought Ben along, and we would like for you to come over."

And I said, "Well the only free time I've got is Sunday morning." I really didn't have any clothes except to go to parties, so I put on what I was going to wear that afternoon to the tea dance, and that was the era of your great big skirts that come within five inches of the floor, a big full-circle skirt with crinoline underneath. It was black with gold dots, and I had a black top on. Ben told me later he was not impressed. I looked overdressed, he said. And I was not impressed with him because he didn't really have anything much to say. He sat there and talked about a *LIFE* magazine he was looking at, so that we had to look at it together—all that morning, looking through some damn... I don't even remember what.

The only reason there was a second date was because Jim had a birthday and Anna's folks had a cabin out in the woods. Out where you go down Creedmoor, on the right, there was this pond—I don't know if it's still there or not—and there was a little road that was just wide enough to get one car through with a body slung over the front like a deer. I don't know why we didn't all get killed. Nobody really paid much attention to safety. I guess when the guys had all been shot at for so long, being veterans, this seemed like a pretty safe environment. Of course, you couldn't drive fast on that road no matter what you were doing; you just stayed in the ruts.

Anna and Jim had their first child. That child was to be baptized the next day, and Ben and I were to be the godparents. I was to go and help Anna get ready for the party, and I was dating Howard's brother Gil, I believe, who later became an architect here in town. Gil had also been dating some girl whose name escapes me but her father, she told me, invented a pig. He must have been something in the Agricultural Department at NC State.

There was no power out there at the time and just an outhouse. No electric lights—there were lamps and a wood stove for cooking. There was a big kitchen and a huge table, and everybody who came brought a bottle and put it on the table. And there were people who brought ice and water.

Anyway, I gave Jim a bottle of white rum for the party, and after making rum balls, there wasn't much to do with the rum. It didn't make good drinks.

Incidentally, the recipe for rum balls, which I learned from my mother, came from Mrs. Josephus Daniels. Josephus Daniels was the man who took rum away from the Navy in World War I. I think he was secretary for the Navy when Roosevelt was the undersecretary. It was his wife's recipe for rum balls. That was *the* rum ball recipe in Raleigh. You could smell them across the room, they were so full of rum.

So Anna and I decided to play a trick on Jim. We emptied out the rum and filled the bottle with vinegar—white vinegar. At some point, Ben and I were sitting together, and we overheard some girl say, "Honey, go get me another one of those rum and Cokes, and this time put more rum in it. That last one tasted just like vinegar."

I can just hear her voice. It was like a made-up Southern accent. She was as Southern as people think that Southerners sound. It was almost a parody she was so Southern—with her rum and Coke. I don't know who she was, but she was there with someone who was in the Order of the Golden Bear at Chapel Hill, who was actually sponsoring the party. The Order of the Golden Bear was primarily made up of vets because they were not only several years older than the entering freshmen, but, let's face it, a lot more mature than they would have been otherwise at that age. It was sort of like a fraternity.

Ben knew that I had brought that white rum bottle filled with white vinegar, and we had such a laugh over this. The party began to break up, and suddenly there was nobody left there. I don't remember if Gil took this girl home whose father invented a pig. All I know is that Ben and Jimmy and Anna and I were the only ones there, and it was four o'clock in the morning. So I called my parents and said, "There's nobody here who's really sober enough to drive me home." I was probably nineteen or twenty.

And my father said, "Well, you just do what everybody else is doing." I think I caught him while he was asleep. He didn't want to drive out there and get me.

The next morning, the only thing left when we finally ended up cleaning up was a watermelon and a bottle of vodka. So we put a hole in the watermelon and poured the bottle of vodka in it, and we had that for breakfast. We were in shape to get Jim's son Jay baptized though. He became a lawyer up in Charlottesville.

Anyway, that did it. The next time Ben came, I dated Ben, and on our third date, he said that I was going to marry him. He would write me letters that had these wonderful drawings, cartoons about whatever had been going on. I do remember one he did that had him sitting on a hill, howling at the moon, and his mother down the hill at the house saying, "I'm sorry, but I can't do a thing with him since he met that girl in Raleigh."

He would come up from Charlotte—and those were all two-lane roads back then—and stay with the Slacks in Raleigh or with a cousin of mine who had a house on St. Mary's Street that's since been torn down. The Arts Together building is there now. It had these towers that were brick, and Ben would stay up in one of those towers.

It was after Ben said that he was going to marry me that I finished college. I graduated from Richmond Professional Institute College of William and Mary in 1948. It's now part of Virginia Commonwealth University. All of the sewing that we were taught at RPI was called

"French finishing." These couture houses had women who did this fine finishing, embroidering that's all hand-done, so that every stitch has to be exactly perfect and all that sort of thing, and we figured that we could get jobs doing that. We had portfolios of samples of doing all this sort of thing, embroidery and quilting, plus the fact that we had taken years of pattern drafting, hours of it. I know five different ways to put in a zipper and things like that. So I came back home and opened a little custom clothing place on Oberlin Road, near where the Player's Retreat bar is.

It was talked about in my family a little bit, me having that business. "Doug has made a job for herself," they said. Some of my friends were in college and got married right away, and some got wonderful educations and then worked taking people's reservations for an airplane ticket; in other words they weren't really doing what they had been trained to do. I think of one in particular who did that. She graduated from Salem and afterwards worked in Washington taking reservations for an airline. She ended up as a librarian and ultimately was the librarian for some sort of Spanish organization that was promoting business in the United States. It was a very specialized library that she had to set up.

Then she had a job at last that really matched her training in library science.

I designed clothes for debutantes and doll clothes. This was before Barbie dolls, and you couldn't really buy nice doll clothes, so I would take the scraps to make them. My cousin Kennon worked with me, and we were making more on our doll clothes than we were on our debutantes.

Raleigh was a little town, and North Carolina was much more class-conscious. Things like the debutante balls were a way for "nice" girls to meet "nice" boys. I know in Warrenton they would have Hospitality Week. Boys from "good old" Southern families and girls from "good old" Southern families would be invited to Warrenton, and there would be parties in the afternoon and dances at night. *LIFE* magazine even covered this one time.

Most Southern states have some sort of similar thing. Some of the cities in North Carolina still have, and did have, separate ones, but the Terpsichorean Society really did pick the *créme de la créme* from across the state. Usually the governor's daughter led the ball. If you were in the figure, which was a kind of formal dance between young men and women, you were the former governor's grandchild or something like that; you had real deep North Carolina roots.

This Friend You Ought to Marry

The Terpsichoreans are still active today. There is still a debutante ball and there is a black debutante ball, and the black ball is interesting the way it works. The girls raise money for scholarship funds, and the girl who raises the most money is the leader. The next ones are the figure, and then the money is divided up among those girls. That still goes on. They put out a beautiful program with all the girls' pictures in it in their debutante dresses.

The black debutantes are not selected by the Terpsichoreans, but there are black old families that are just as protective of their old family connections—the Turners, the Rothschilds down on Oberlin Road, the Popes who owned all the land in Macon. They were always free. They were descended from one of the Boylans and an Indian woman from down in Wilmington, and when he died, he left the children all that land that is now Method and it still has come down through the family. It is divided up so that there are so many houses over there now.

During the war, the debutante ball was not held. Some of the girls who would have made their debut did make it later. Most did not. I had one or two friends who made their debut after the war, one very good friend, and I'm pretty sure she made her debut because her two sisters had, and her family felt that she would be shorted if they didn't do that for her.

Very frankly, if I had wanted to, I could have. I did not make my debut. I did not want to. My stated reason for that was, of course, that it had been during the war. My reason might have been different if it had not been during the war.

Anyway, I went to deb parties that they held in the years after World War II. The last debutante party I went to, which was the last debutante ball I went to, I had created the gown for one of the debs. Really, if you were anybody in Raleigh, you should go to Willie Kay for your dress. She came to me instead of Willie Kay, so I don't know quite how she got in, but I got an invitation.

Ben had been coming up about every other weekend to see me at the time, and he said, no, he couldn't go to the debutante ball with me. He just couldn't get into tails and do that. Well, I didn't say anything about it. I knew that he kept coming every other weekend, so I didn't make an issue of it. I just borrowed some tails from one of my cousins, and when he came that weekend, I said, "You know, I've got these tickets and here's these tails..."

The pants had to be shortened, so someone called over to the Slacks, and Pop Slack, who was the father of my friend Anna Slack—everybody called her father "Pop"—anyway Pop answered the phone, and I heard him say, "Yeah, Doug's back in the sewing room turning up Ben's pants, which is probably better than Ben back there turning up her skirt."

Anyway, when Ben eventually proposed, I sort of laughed it off. I wasn't ready to commit then. I guess it was the next spring that he said, "I want to talk to your dad." We had been dating for a year by that time, and my parents really thought he was one of the nicest and most responsible young men I had gone out with. He was looking after his mother and his younger brother when he got back from the army. At that time he had not gone back to college. Instead he was working for Amoco in their engineering department as a secretary. Ultimately, he was recommended by one of the engineers in the company to go work as a steel estimator. And he never did go back to college. I think he was in college about six weeks before he went into the military.

He talked to my father, and my father said, "I have nothing to say," or as Ben used to put it, my father objected when he started talking about making an honest woman out of me. My parents liked him as a person. All their friends liked him. They thought Ben was an awfully nice person for me to go out with, one of the nicest people I had ever gone out with, but they did not know a thing about his family. They didn't know who Ben's people were. Here is this man whose father is from Germany, and you just can't tell about these immigrants. Now, his mother was old North Carolina. Her grandfather had been a lieutenant governor of North Carolina, but she is from the Piedmont, and we are not kin to many people there. Most people married somebody they were already connected to.

I was mad. I thought this was ridiculous. So, the next time Ben came up, after he spoke with my father, we decided we would get married the next weekend; it was payday. That was what determined our wedding date. I took the bus to Charlotte. He made the arrangements for us to be married at Avondale Presbyterian Church. There was just his family. One of Ben's old girlfriends came and sat in the back and wept copiously all the way through the service. His mother Shorty had a little reception at her house after. She said, "Brides should have something nice to remember for their wedding day."

We got married in 1950. We had been married six years before my father even visited us. My mother came around immediately. We would go to visit my parents, but my father would always go play golf when we did.

<u>Chapter Five</u>
The Bottom of Their Pockets

Ben at that time owned his mother's house on Park Road. He had used his GI loan to get the house remodeled. His younger brother was still in high school. His older brother had come back from the military and decided the best thing to do with the house was tear it down and sell the land. Ben knew that would be very upsetting for Shorty. I think she was agoraphobic before people knew what that was, and she became this after Ben's father died or probably even earlier than that. The fact that they lost so much during the Depression was hard on her.

We were using the refrigerator that my mother bought with the first money she had ever made. She bought it for her mother. It was a GE with what Thurber used to call "the doom-shaped thing" on top, which was the condenser. Well, the one we had did not have a "doom" shape. Ours was just a big coil, and it quit on us a couple of times. The refrigerator man came out the first time it quit, and he said we could buy a new one and he would give us credit for the coil, but what it really needed was for the motor to be shaken. The thing weighed a ton, so Ben took the back end of a hatchet and hit it, and it started right up. Anytime the thing quit after that, he would hit it, until finally that refrigerator once just saw Ben walk across the kitchen holding that hatchet and it started.

One of the things I've always found interesting about Park Road down in Charlotte is three men who grew up on Park Road within a mile of each other. One is Ben and one is Billy Graham and one is Jack Spong. Spong is a Bishop in the Episcopal Church who was the first bishop to marry a gay couple. He's considered very, very Liberal. Ben was kind of in the middle of these two ministers in age. Billy Graham was the same age as Ben's older brother, so he's about five years older, and Jack was our paper boy, so he was about five years younger.

I know the Spongs and the Haases were friends and probably on the same social level. Jack's mother was an Associate Reform Presbyterian, which is a very Conservative branch of Presbyterianism that was quite strong in Charlotte. His father was an Episcopalian, which was how he ended up being an Episcopalian. Ben's parents I don't think were involved in church particularly, but they certainly had the same middle-class values.

Then Billy Graham's father had a dairy down the road. He lived the farthest away and is always referred to in that area of Charlotte as Billy Frank. My mother never called him anything but Billy Frank. Billy Frank Graham was his name. I think they were probably Baptist, and I believe Billy Frank was converted or saved at a Moody Revival. I don't know a whole lot about them. I just know that their dairy farm was not held in as high esteem as Ashcroft's, which was between their house and the Spongs. During World War II the Grahams dairy had been cited for watering their milk. But he went off in a different direction and certainly made a name for himself.

Anyway, we probably lived there on Park Road a few months, and then Ben and I rented an apartment on Providence Road that was in a four-unit building owned by a Greek couple. At that time, Ben said every restaurant in Charlotte was owned by the Greeks, even the Chinese ones. We were living there when Joel was born. It was just down the street from the Presbyterian hospital. When we moved in, the only furniture we had was the Murphy bed that came with the apartment— one of these beds that used to fold up in the wall, the kind they used to do lots of comic things with in the early movies. Laurel and Hardy almost always had somebody in a Murphy bed.

A little later, Ben and I moved into a place out in the country on Shearin View Road. It had been a little play house, and the people who had lived there had built it to use in summer for parties. It had a nice porch, and during the war, people were being encouraged to make more places for people to live. So the man who owned it added two bedrooms, a bath, and a kitchen. And we rented it.

I didn't transfer my business to Charlotte, but I did put an ad in the paper there for several years, saying I could make doll clothes for people on special order for Christmas. I don't think anybody really considered dress-making a business.

The first real selling job I ever had, I worked at Johnny's Hobby House in Charlotte in the early '50s. It was a toy store before chain toy stores, sort of the FAO Schwartz of the South. It was owned by a man named Johnny Vogler, and Johnny told us all that we sold things that nobody had to have. Years later, I looked at my costume shop, Raleigh Creative Costumes, in sort of the same way. I didn't sell anything that, unless you were in the theater, you had to have.

The Bottom of Their Pockets

So we were to play with the toys, make them look like fun. And if there was no customer in the store, we were to stand in the window and play with something, get people interested to come in. Johnny had a company too, what they call "secret shoppers," and they would come in and buy things and then write a report on how we had sold and whether we had "found the bottom of their pockets."

Ben got a job with General Foods. General Foods had just come out with instant coffee and sugar-coated cereals. Ben loved selling instant coffee. There were not that many big chain grocery stores then. Piggly Wiggly I guess was the biggest. The whole idea was that he would go into these little country grocery stores, and they usually had a kettle of water on their pot-bellied stove, so he'd say, "Get a cup, and I'll show you." And he'd stir them up a cup of instant Maxwell House coffee, which was the first instant that came along. And they would be so impressed that they would buy lots of instant coffee from him.

The other thing, though, that they wanted him to sell were these sugar-coated cereals. Krinkles, I believe they were called. They had test-marketed these up North, and they had been just hugely popular. So General Foods thought, well, this would be good to sell in the South and all over the country, and Ben had made such good relations because of all of that instant coffee that he sold more sugar-coated cereal than anybody else in the Southeast, cases and cases of it, hundreds of cases of it.

This would have been probably in the wintertime, in January or so, because Joel would not have been walking yet. But as the warmer weather came along, Ben began to have grocery men who were complaining because the boxes of cereal were solid now. This was before air-conditioning. The sugar had melted in the heat and that had solidified these boxes.

So Ben asked his boss at General Foods, what to do about this, and his boss called headquarters, and headquarters said, "Well, if you just take the boxes and hit them on your knee, they'll break up. Show all the grocery men how to do this."

Well, he went around to all these little grocery stores and told them how to break up the cereal boxes by hitting them. Within a week, of course, all of those had re-solidified, and the grocery men were getting testy about spending most of their time breaking boxes of cereal over their knees.

Again the word went out to the head office, "What do we do?"

And the head office said, "I guess it's back to the old drawing board. If you would just refund the money that all these grocery men have spent with General Foods and then cut off the tops of the boxes and send us the tops of the boxes, we will refund you."

So Ben would bring these cases home, a few at a time. I can remember it got to the point that the little room Joel had for a bedroom, which just had his crib in there, was stacked to the ceiling with cases of sugar-coated cereal. Every day, while Ben was out selling coffee and picking up more boxes, I spent the day sitting out on the front porch, with Joel on a little blanket in the yard, and I would cut the tops off of these boxes to try to get money back for them.

Well, then we had to get rid of hundreds and thousands of boxes of cereal that were now bricks. I found a woman who worked in some of the houses around the neighborhood there who lived on a farm down the road. She said her husband raised hogs, and they'd take that cereal and feed it to the hogs. They did, until the vet told them that the hogs' kidneys were failing because they had gotten too much sugar in their diet.

Finally we just had to build up a big bonfire out behind the house. We kept adding boxes to the fire every day as I cut the box tops off, so it burned, as I recall, for about three days, emitting great plumes of sugar-smelling smoke into the neighborhood.

By the time we went down to Sumter, SC, Michael had been born. John was born in Sumter, while we lived there. Ben was working at the B. L. Montague steel company, which is a big structural steel company. He was chief estimator and assistant sales manager for them, and we lived in a house in a rented area of town that we were the only civilians in. There was a huge base there, and so all of our neighbors were military people who had just moved to Sumter.

When we moved to Sumter, incidentally, they moved us into the wrong house. The movers came, packed everything up, and I took the animals. We, at that time, had a dog and a cat and a rabbit, and two children, and Ben was already in Sumter, working and staying at a motel, and I was to arrive with the children and the animals. We stayed at the motel that first night with Ben, but the next morning I loaded up the children and the animals and went over to number 24 Meadow Circle to wait for the movers. I remember that day. It was in the spring and Sumter was absolutely beautiful. They have a lovely iris garden there with all these swans on a pond, so it was very enticing, and we thought, "Oh, this would be a beautiful place to live."

The Bottom of Their Pockets

The movers never came. Along about two o'clock in the afternoon, the little pick-up truck from the moving company drove up and the driver said, "You know, we have unloaded you at number 24 Meadowbrook Circle, which was empty, but because there was no refrigerator there and you weren't there with all those animals, we began to worry about this."

Sure enough, they had moved us in the wrong house. Not only that, it was a Wednesday, and at that time a lot of people had Wednesday afternoons off, so the owner of the Red Ball franchise that was moving us was the only person still working. All of his crew was left, and he had to do it all by himself. I remember that Ben came home that night and went out and got a bottle of vodka and came back and helped the guy.

We really had little interchange with the people in Sumter. The only thing was we went to a church supper at the Episcopal Church. We were invited there because my uncle used to preach there sometimes, and some old man entertained by playing the saw, I remember. One of the ladies in the church gave a history of the church, and you could hear her, as she talked about "the Enemy" turning the church sanctuary into a hospital, it was as if the Union Army were at the door knocking right then.

Her Words

When I would pick up my groceries down at the little country store, there would often be a flyer in there telling where the Klan was gathering and having their cross burning this weekend and inviting people. And I did see crosses burned. I would be driving down the road and see them.

The White Citizens Council was something that was more or less everywhere. They were not a part of the Klan—no violence. These were the businessmen in town who could see the impact that integration would have. They would have to start hiring blacks, which would increase competition for white workers. We just didn't realize how much more serious they were about it in South Carolina.

School integration had already been passed in Congress, that the schools would be integrated "with all deliberate speed," and everybody in South Carolina, more than almost anywhere else, was dragging their feet. If the federal government wanted to integrate the schools, the White Citizen's Council would make sure South Carolina was going to close its schools. They certainly looked like they were going to because they hadn't put any money in them, black or white, but they built a private school for white children who could afford it.

The Bottom of Their Pockets

I had one neighbor who was a first-grade teacher in public school, and she talked about how it was just really bad—that they had no supplies, the buildings were in bad shape, and she was worried about her own children. She was more or less homeschooling them, really, so that the next time they were transferred somewhere else, the children wouldn't be so behind. And at that time, the military was very segregated, so these were all white members of the military living in the area. The White Citizen's Council were biting off their nose to spite their faces.

There was a Catholic school right across the street from B. L. Montague. It was actually an old house that was probably antebellum, which several nuns lived in and ran a little school, kindergarten through third grade. And so we investigated that school. We found that the school existed to a great extent to school the children of the military, because there weren't that many Catholics in town.

One time two mothers came to me one day and said, "Doug, we want you to go with us to the father and talk to him. They're talking about not having a sister for third grade."

And I said, "Well, I don't really think that I'm the person to go. I'm Presbyterian."

And one of them women said, "Well, I'm Methodist."

And the other one said, "I'm Baptist." So that was the end of the committee.

The school has survived, by the way. I had an order from them at the costume shop several years ago. It was really strange. I got this call from Sumter, SC, and the woman said, "This is for a little primary school, St. Anne's."

And I said, "Oh, I know St. Anne's!"

So we entered Joel in St. Anne's school, which also didn't endear us to the population because they knew that the Catholics were for integration. We were sleeping with the enemy, so to speak. There had been a prejudice against Catholics before integration came up, and the Catholic priests often supported marches and whatnot. After all, they weren't dependent on a congregation for support. In fact, Episcopalians supported integration more openly than most churches simply because they were more dependent on their bishop to protect them from their congregation. They are ruled from the top down. So if your bishop supported you, the congregation might fight like crazy what you were preaching to them, but your job was secure. Now in the Baptist church, however, ministers used to say that they never preached without a resignation statement stationed in their pocket.

We were targeted after Ben didn't join the White Citizens Council. One day he was sitting in his office and there a delegation from the company came to call on him. The man said, "Boy, I know you've got a new baby in your house. If it's the two dollars, we'll put up the money, but we want our company to go a hundred percent for the council." I quote him because I think it's interesting how he used the word "boy." Two dollars was the membership fee.

When Ben refused their two dollars, he was told, "Well, maybe we should pay a little visit some night."

And Ben said, "Well, you know, that'll be interesting because my house is down on the Sand Flat outside of town, and my neighbors on both sides just happen to be military policemen." Certainly our next-door neighbors were not going to put up with this stuff. And he and Joel at the time knew how to use a gun, in case that should be necessary. So they never showed up. They never burned a cross in our yard.

Chapter Six
Writer in Residence
at the Player's Retreat

We were very pleased when Ben got an offer to come up to Raleigh to work. We felt like it was a little more civilized. We could buy *The New York Times* on Sundays. We used to not get it in Sumter until Tuesday and sometimes Wednesday. And if you wanted a book other than the Bible or the dictionary, you had to drive to Columbia.

Wat came back to Raleigh too. She had a lot of time to do well in New York, but I think that, after her son Frank was born, she didn't want to live how she would have to live, and she could come back home and have a nurse to look after Frank and someone to cook and wash for her. She wouldn't have to do any housekeeping and, like me, had never had to growing up. I probably only had to do a little more than she had, but I would say that most girls of our level and our age in the South then did not have a lot of housekeeping skills.

In fact, I can remember I had never washed anything when I got to Mars Hill. I was sixteen, and I had a blouse that I really liked. They had little cases that you sent laundry home in, brown cases with straps on them that the post office knew were for laundry, and then it was sent back to you, all washed and ironed. This was just a standard for all college kids to get their laundry done. There were no washing machines in the buildings. So these cases were especially made for sending your laundry back and forth. But I wanted to wear this blouse and it was dirty. Some of the girls at Mars Hill knew more about this than I did. I wasn't going to admit that I didn't know, so I spent one Saturday afternoon down in the basement washroom, a whole afternoon washing this one blouse, watching how the others starched and ironed things like this. And that's how I learned to wash and starch and iron.

So it wasn't unusual for someone like Wat not to have the housekeeping skills that would have gotten her through living in an apartment in New York with a baby and a husband who might be out on the road, while she was auditioning somewhere. And her father died at about that time, which meant that her mother would be alone.

I think Wat took great pride in making and earning money while her father was alive, rather than spending Daddy's money, because by Raleigh standards at that time he was quite well off. I remember she had a coat, a red coat, that she told me, "I paid for this with my own money."

She made a big splash at Raleigh Little Theater when she returned. Doris Dworsky talked about this at Wat's funeral, about how she was intimidated with the training that Wat had, because they both would try out for similar parts. And Wat was a good actress.

She wasn't telling anybody how old she was, but everybody knew that she and I had been friends and that we had been in school together. She said, "Doug, everybody thinks I'm twenty-five, so don't say how old you are."

And I said, "Well, Wat, that's ok, but it's awfully hard to explain how I have a twelve-year-old child." She and I were both about thirty-two at the time. This would have been in 1958.

Dick Snavely was directing a production of *The Lark* and Wat suggested that I might make patterns for the clothes they needed. At that time there were no standard clothing patterns for various period costumes. I had all along occasionally done a costume for one person or another, very often for Wat. Even before we both came back to Raleigh, I was still doing costumes for her. And so that was the first thing I did for the theater. I never costumed a whole show while the children were really little, but from that point on I would be involved with many shows in one way or another.

And making doll clothes was sort of like doing costumes for theater, because you tell the doll what it has to wear. As the costumer in a theater, you have a great deal of power over seeing what is to be worn, whether they like that color or not. I remember one actor who wanted a costume that would match his baby blue eyes. And I said, "If I find any blue fabric." Actually in that particular show he did wear blue, but in *A Midsummer Night's Dream*, he played Puck, and I put him in green.

Guy Munger, like Ben, looked like an unmade bed most of the time. I dressed him once for a Pinter play, *A Delicate Balance*. Harry Callahan was directing it, and Harry said, "Doug, could you have a dresser to stand in the wing, and every time Guy comes off, have them spray him with a can of spray starch?"

When we moved to Raleigh, Guy and Joan had just moved there themselves from Hawaii, where Guy had been a reporter for a local paper. Before then, Jim Henderson had worked with them both at *The Greensboro Daily News* and he wrote and said we ought to get in touch.

Writer in Residence at the Player's Retreat

We saw Joan in a play—I can't remember which play it was—and went backstage afterwards and said to Joan, "Do you know Jim Henderson?"

And she said, "Why do you want to know?" From that point on, we became friends with the Mungers.

There's one funny story about them selling their car when they left Hawaii. It was pouring rain the day that a Chinese gentleman came who seemed really interested in buying and wanted to ride in the car. So they had to keep up the windows. Of course, there was no air conditioning in cars then.

At that time if you had five small children, three of whom are still in diapers, you could put three people in the front and three in the back seat, or do what Ben and I did. We had a bench that was exactly the level of the back seat so that it just made a big area like a playpen back there. Actually, we had bought our car from Jim and Anna Henderson. They had the bench built because they had a bunch of kids too, five children, with the youngest one born on the oldest one's fifth birthday.

Well, after these un-house-broken Munger children had been riding in Guy and Joan's car for a year, it was not a good idea to ride in the car with the windows all up, especially if you are trying to sell the car. And the man who was testing the car with Guy, at the end of the ride, he said, "Ah, a family car, I believe..." We all had "family cars" in those days, before disposable diapers.

In Raleigh, they were living in a house that has since been torn down. It was owned by the Proctors on New Bern Avenue. I think there is a historic marker there. But the house was a wonderful big old house and had lots of furniture in it. Even then Joan was addicted to shopping at auctions.

They had a big console television which was put in what been the ballroom at the Proctor house. And Joan bought what had been an old shoe shine stand, which was a line of seats with arms between them and numbers on them, from what had been the old Yarborough Hotel before it burned down. This was also bought at auction. I think she paid twenty-five cents for it. She put the shoe shine stand in the ballroom for the kids to sit in to watch TV. Bridget was born while they were living there, so that was six children then.

Joan did some freelance work. I remember the 1960 census. Wat and I worked for her, taking the census, and that was really interesting.

We were supposed to interview all the visitors that were in any home we entered, and I'll never forget the day that Wat called me and said, "What do you think?" It was the day that Wat had an area on Oberlin Road, and she said that when she talked to the lady who kept a boarding house for young girls, the lady said, "No there is no one here today," but Wat said she could see a man leaving out the back.

Guy wrote a story for this. He was also a stringer for *Newsweek* at the time, so he wrote a story they published about some of the problems census takers would encounter.

Wat and I were assigned for any problems finding people. One man I found when finally I got him on the telephone one night. There was a long form and a short form for the census. In the long form, you asked a lot of questions. Things like, "How many bathrooms are in your house?" Or, "How many siblings do you have?" One of them though was about their job, and I asked this man what his job was. He said he worked at Rex Hospital. And I said, "What is your job at Rex Hospital?"

And he said, "I's the floatin' boy."

And I said, "What does the 'floatin' boy' do at Rex Hospital?"

And he said, "I just floats from flo' to flo'." I don't know how that was ultimately classified as a job.

I also went to houses where people had dogs because I have a way with dogs. My secret was I always called the dog and said, "Here, pup! Here, pup! Come here, pup! Nice dog!" And I held my hand there to sniff. The master would be standing there, looking at the dog, saying, "Sick 'em! Sick 'em!" And the dog would be standing there, all smiles.

They would have sicked the dog on the last census taker, so that was a problem house. There are just some people who don't want the government to know they exist. I'm sure there are still some people like that. Maybe he's making moonshine in the back, or nowadays maybe he's doing some drug. He doesn't want anybody from the government there.

We met a lot of the newspaper people and theater people through the Mungers and Wat and the parties that they would have, big parties with lots of people coming. They were wonderful parties. There might be fifty to seventy-five there, all very interesting people. And interesting people attract more interesting people, especially if you have booze out or say, "Bring your own bottle." In those days, that was a very common thing, to bring your own bottle.

In fact, women always had a purse that was big enough to at least hold a pint, and preferably a fifth, because you couldn't buy mixed drinks when you went out to eat. This was in the '40s and '50s. But you could buy a set up. They brought you glasses and maybe soft drinks and a big bowl of ice with lemons all over it. That was a set up. And the women had brought the liquor in their purses. It made an interesting side line of clothing, the fact that you had to have a purse that you could fit this in that was still a dress-up purse to go out, none of these little evening bags you see women carrying nowadays. And you couldn't buy those little bottles either. You either bought a fifth or a pint.

Dee Williams I remember meeting at the time out there at what we called a "Mungering." Dee was secretary of the International Rolls Royce Club and drove an old Rolls Royce. I think he finally sold it when he had to go into assisted living. And Mickey and Bernie Hanula from the Player's Retreat. Bernie had been a star football player for NC State. At that time, they were up in a little place on Hillsborough Street at Dan Allen Drive, right at the stop light across from the textile building. That was the original Player's

Retreat. This was before Player's Retreat moved down to the corner of Hillsborough and Oberlin.

At these parties, there would be teachers from the university and some of the grad students. Most of these were foreign grad students who probably had come because one of their teachers had said, "You'll get to meet a lot of real Americans." It's just as today. If you travel, it's always nice to be invited into a foreigner's home, and it's nice to invite foreigners in. That sort of thing is always good. It works both ways.

One of the Munger parties is where we met two grad students, P. K. Mitra and Carlos Pontiac. P. K. was from India, and they were sitting in the kitchen at the Proctor House when P. K. said something about the Sepoy Rebellion. It was when the Indians rose up against the British. Ben was in there, and he talked with him about the Sepoy Rebellion, and P. K. said, "You're the first American I've known who ever knew anything about this." From that, we became friends. He and Carlos were looking for another place to live. They didn't like where they were living, and we had just rented this house on Bedford Avenue that had an apartment upstairs that had a separate entrance and all. And so we said, "Well, if you want to rent our apartment..." So they became our tenants and close friends.

P. K. was very dark and, at that time, would sometimes be refused service. And Ben asked him why he did not wear a turban, because turban-wearing Indians had never seemed to have any problem in the South, and P. K. said, no, that he didn't wear a turban. That was the first time we realized that the turban was part of a religious thing.

And he surprised us when his family called him and told him they had found him a nice wife. P. K. went back to India and had a traditional Indian wedding. She had a PhD. I forget in what. Their marriage was not a good one, but they stayed together.

Erna and Jack Mirza had come to the States to study, and she was a Zoroastrian, just like the three wise men. They were the magi from the East. We think of them as kings, but they weren't kings. They were just learned men from the East.

Anyway, Jack was a sort of Universalist, and they had gotten married. He was in school at State, and her parents had suggested or his parents had suggested that they should meet, so he went up to meet her.

Jack was in the electrical engineering department at State, one of the few times that somebody who had gotten all the way through to PhD they kept. He was very highly thought of there. When he died, very young, the funeral was interesting. His brother was a concert pianist in Germany, so he arranged for somebody to play Beethoven's sonatas, and somebody read something from the Bible, the Psalms, and somebody else read from the Koran. It was a rather interesting funeral. It was held at the University ballroom.

Erna had studied in India with Madame Montessori. During the Second World War, Madame Montessori was teaching a sort of one-year fellowship in India, and the war came on and she couldn't get back. So she stayed and just kept teaching. So before Erna came to the States, she had studied child development and care "right from the horse's mouth," so to speak. And she used a lot of those techniques. They had a little girl, Zimina, who my son John played with a lot because they just lived across the street from us, and he loved to play there because they had all these interesting things to do with water and cut-out numbers to play with and things like that, long before educational toys were quite the big thing they are now.

They lived across the street from us in Bedford Avenue, and they ended up buying a house in the streets behind us, on Van Dyke, so they were still always in the neighborhood, over by Fred Olds. A lot of foreign students lived in the neighborhood. I know there was a little boy who was Korean, and he was already a quite advanced piano student, because his mother was a pianist, and he used to come to our house and he and Mike would play piano together. Last I heard, he was teaching at Peabody.

Ben went with Erna and Jack to get their citizenship on the snowiest day in North Carolina you can imagine. They had to go down to Fayetteville to be sworn in as American citizens. We were also their sponsors.

Our sons were enrolled at Fred Olds school, just as I had been. All three of my boys went to Fred Olds. My son John mentioned that he was talking to his group at work about the South being a sort of enclave, and he said, "My mother, my brothers, and I all went to the same school. In fact, we all sat in the same fifth grade classroom with the same fifth grade teacher."

That teacher was real funny when Joel came into class. She said her mother told her, "All right, when you start teaching the second generation, it's time to quit, Virginia." But she taught a lot of second-generation kids over there at Fred Olds.

I remember the first black teacher who came to Fred Olds worked in the library, and I volunteered in the library. She floated from school to school, and what a lovely person she was, as if she had been raised by any white upper-class family. I remember hearing one of the teachers comment that she was very upset there was being a "colored" librarian, of course. It was interesting to see how she changed the attitude of the teachers who were there by the end of the year. I remember that same teacher eventually saying in admiration, "Look at how the children cluster around her wherever she is."

Ben was always writing, and occasionally during the years, I think before he even went in the military, he had sold a story to *Forty-Four Westerns*, which was really what he always wanted to do, do nothing but write westerns. But nobody much was publishing westerns then except as pulp fiction. This was long before *Lonesome Dove* and that sort of thing ever came out, so he never really had the chance to write a serious western, which is too bad because that was really what he would have like to have done.

Ben had been sending manuscripts around almost as long as I had known him, and they would almost invariably be returned with a little noted that said, "Dear Mr. Haas, your manuscript generated a great deal of interest in our office..." So I used to tease him. I called him "The Interest Generator."

Finally, when we had moved to Raleigh, he said he was reading a paperback book and he realized, "Hey, I could write this with both hands behind my back, practically." So he wrote three chapters and an outline and started sending it. He was just going to go down the list, and when he sent it to Belmont, they contacted him and said, "Could you write six books like this in a year?" He knew it hadn't taken him very long to write that. I think they were offering $1000 a manuscript even then, and that was better than he was making where he was, particularly since his present employer's checks were bouncing. So he accepted and said, yes, he would.

He signed a contract and then he called Scott Meredith. Ben read a lot of the magazines such as *The Writer's Digest*, all of these, and he saw that Scott seemed to be actually doing things with his writers. He called Scott's office and said, "I will give you the commission on these six books," because at that time I think you had to have $1500 worth of writing before they would take you on as a percentage, and this was $6000.

Within three days, Scott had placed Ben's manuscript for *The Foragers*, a hard cover he had been sending around, with Simon & Schuster, because Scott knew who needed a book on the Civil War that was that length. Lots of times, it's a matter of knowing who needs what length of book on what subject. Everybody else had written back, "We have a major Southern novel coming out this year, and in our fall and in our spring so we don't need another one."

The Foragers had gone around and Ben had gotten a lot of suggestions from these friends of my uncle Doug's. He had made a lot of the changes that they had suggested. I remember him telling me about the second chapter. It was about a group of Confederate soldiers on a foraging party who had taken a calf from an old woman who lived up in the mountains and whose husband had gone off to fight in "the rich man's war with the poor man's fight." She was trying to feed two children at home and farm. He said he saw the whole thing. He was stopped at a stop light in Sumter when we were living there, and suddenly this whole thing came before his eyes, and he came home that night and wrote what ultimately became the second chapter of the book.

So, *The Foragers* came out. It had a full-page ad in the New York Times review of books, so he had good publicity right from the start. And at that point he was making enough writing paperbacks, sometimes these paperbacks that he ghosted for somebody else. I remember Abby Mann did a movie called *A Child is Waiting*, and

Writer in Residence at the Player's Retreat

Ben ghost-wrote the book that came out afterward that was supposed to be the book that the movie was taken from. Manly Wade Wellman was writing science fiction and westerns then, and I remember how Manly and Ben used to laugh about how Manly said he would have written every one of the stories in this one science fiction magazine under different names, and the same thing happened to Ben when he was writing so many paperback westerns. He said he'd look on a bookshelf in the drugstore or something, and everything on there either he or Louis L'Amour had written under various names. I'm sure Louis L'Amour wrote under some other names too.

Ben was known as "the writer in residence" at the Player's Retreat because, for a good bit of his time in Raleigh, his office was in that building up over the Retreat. He had the office that was on the corner that has the little balcony that goes on it. There's some apartments up there. Florence King, another writer, also had a place there, as did Brian Shawcroft and Dee Williams. But when Ben had his office up there, he didn't want to be disturbed, so he didn't have a telephone. If anyone wanted him, they called the Retreat and someone from the went upstairs and told him he was wanted on the phone.

Then he got an advance to do *Look Away, Look Away*, based on what he told Simon and Schuster about Maggie, my family's housekeeper who was related to the editor of *The Wall Street Journal* who later became editor of *The News & Observer*. Kennedy was shot in the fall and it was published the next spring, and that was when we moved to Austria the first time.

The people who read Ben's book see a very Liberal view—a Southern Liberal's view—of the South at that time. We are all a part of our heritage, a part of our time, and what's Liberal in one time won't be Liberal in another, or maybe what was considered Liberal in 1930s is not considered Liberal in 1960. We got a call from some fraternity down in Mississippi who wanted to know if *Look Away, Look Away* was going to be some other Yankee garbage that he wouldn't want to read. Ben had lots of letters from people who said, "You could only write this if you were a black man." And then it was really interesting, the letters he got, because he had really picked up on some of the feelings of blacks that they didn't think anybody had heard.

I remember being with Ben when he did some research in Georgia for *Look Away, Look Away* on lynching, and there was this big black man with the name Griff. Ben was telling him what he was doing, and Ben said, "My editor in New York wants to get this book finished because he thinks this is going to be a dead issue in a year or two."

And this guy pushed back his chair and said, "Boy, this won't be a dead issue by the end of the century." I loved the fact that he called Ben "boy." And the other thing was they were talking about how it was just at that time you were beginning to have to put more "e" in "negro" when you were a Southerner.

Ben said, "I kind of have to get a running start to get that much 'e' in it."

And I remember Griff laughing and saying, "I do too!"

Chapter Seven
On the Corner of
Brahms and Franz-Schubert

Ben had taken German in high school, which was unusual because most of the high schools had stopped teaching German. He had signed up, he said, for Spanish, but the Spanish teacher also taught German at the high school in Charlotte and told him that, no, he had no business taking Spanish. Because of his father, he should take German. German hadn't been a hard language for Ben, and at that time Austria and Spain were the two least expensive countries in Europe to live in. Spain was under Franco's rule, and Austria had a reputation for education and good medical facilities—and after all, we had three small boys— so it seemed like the place to try.

When I was younger, I tried, when I got out of college, to get a job on a ship so I could go to Europe. My Aunt Belle, in spite of her trying to get enough "e" in my language, told me that if I could get to Paris to live and work for a year that she would send me a stipend. She had spent a year there as a young girl herself. So I tried to get a job on a ship, but it was not that easy right after the war.

I had always wanted to go to Europe. This was not a leap for me at all. I was about thirty-five when we first picked up the kids and left. We got Mickey Hanula to see to renting the house we had bought on Bedford Avenue—best landlady we ever had.

You no longer could buy steamer trunks new, and we were going by ship because that was the only way to travel then. I remember I bought all the steamer trunks at what Joan Munger and I used to call "the drunk store." It wasn't run by Goodwill, but it was run by some similar organization. They tried to rehabilitate drunks by having them refurbish furniture or appliances or whatnot and to work in the store. Sadly, the drunk store was one of the places that got burned when tensions heated-up over Civil Rights later on. I never could understand why they burned it.

We travelled over by ship and back the first time we went in the '60s. We went over on the Amsterdam. Joel was in middle school and John and Mike were in primary school. John was, as a little boy, walking around, introducing himself to everybody to the point that even decades later in Europe people asked me, "And how is Mr. President?" because he would go up to strangers and say, "I'm John Douglas Haas," and hold out his hand to be shook.

The first time we went, people looked at us like, "What are you doing with these children?" When we first knew that we were going overseas to live, I went to Fred Olds and talked to the principal about what I should take along to keep up the children's math lessons or whatnot, and it was interesting because at that time Fred Olds got most of the kids who came here whose parents were just here for a year. We didn't have the influx yet that started with IBM. It was mostly foreign grad students or professors over at NC State.

And he commented that the children who came in from other countries, it took them about three months. The first thing they would catch onto were the words associated with their math class, which was my children's poorest subject, but it still was the first thing that they caught on to in Austria. They would probably learn the most from their little friends on the street, and within about three months they would be getting along fine, while maybe not scoring the highest of anyone in the class, certainly well within a normal range.

I have letters written by their school after our first sojourn there that talk about that and about the things they were strongest in. There were things they were stronger in than the other children there and things they were weaker in, which was interesting. Their writing was very poor, and the writing in Austria is so beautifully taught. When my children left, the teacher brought a little autograph book and each child, using a pen that would be dipped in ink at the desk, wrote and drew a little picture on every page for the boys, and there was only one blot in all of the books.

The Austrian schools are actually very accustomed to teaching children who don't know German because the Austro-Hungarian Empire was made up of sixteen different languages, and the area we lived in had been occupied by the Russians, so the teachers there had been required to teach in Russian. At the head of the little four-class school where our boys went to, two teachers had actually been teaching in Czechoslovakia. They had been teaching children in Czech, German, and Hungarian, so teaching children in English was just one more.

The *musik gymnasium* is the school that Vienna Boys Choir boys go to when their voices change, because they've been guaranteed an education. Their teaching system is so different from ours. The whole class stays together, and the teacher comes to them. They had already had two years of Latin when my son John came in, so there was no way he was ever going to catch up with that. That was the main thing that he was still behind in, I think. So he came back to the United Sates before Ben and I did. He finished up at the School of the Arts in Winston-Salem.

In Austria, I primarily tended to the home because shopping is a daily chore there, particularly in the '60s. There were no supermarkets. By the time we went back in the '70s, there was a supermarket in Vienna called Pom-Pom, which always amused Ben because "pom-pom" was how sex was referred to in the Philippines where he'd been stationed in World War II.

But in the '60s there were all these little specialty shops, and we had a refrigerator that was about the size of a small safe. It didn't even have a floor. It had this rubber sort of tub in it so that you couldn't stand a bottle of milk up. Everybody who bought milk always put it on the outside of the house or in their basement. The second time we went, we had a refrigerator that did have a little ice compartment, and since you had to pay for everything with cash, I used to keep my cash in there, because nobody but an American would get an ice tray out.

Anyway, I was daily walking to the stores and getting fresh food. I'd go down often. I was just learning German myself then, and the first thing I learned were the names of things. I would go to the grocery store and say, "What's this? And this?" or send the children very often, and since we lived up on the last mountain of the Alps, they developed good leg muscles. I mean, our sidewalk in some places was really just steps. Michael, years later, was having a physical for a recording company for their insurance, and the doctor said, "I don't think I ever saw such leg muscles on a musician."

Helmut Seif became a good friend of Ben's. He got Ben in as a member of the *Klosterneuburgerschootswereim*, which is a shooting club. Ben was the only American member they had ever had. They had a plaque on their wall from the Emperor in 1600-something, thanking them for helping in the defense of Vienna against the Turks.

While we were in Austria the first time, Ben wrote *The Last Valley*. He used the transcript of a utility commission hearing from when the people built Fontana Dam and they were flooding a lot of the old hill country up there in Appalachia. All the advertising was saying how it would provide cheap electricity for the eastern part of the state and encourage the factories to bring new jobs to the area. But when it got down to the nitty-gritty, it turned out that it was all to go to the Alcoa aluminum company in Tennessee, and only the surplus would be available for North Carolinians whose land had all been taken over. So Ben based the book on the rights of Eminent Domain and what it does, and that sort of thing. And one of the things he said living in Austria was that mountain people, whether they were Austrians or Americans, were all very independent people.

Austria also stood in the rather peculiar position that they collected reparations from Germany as one of the overrun countries, even though the *Anschluss*, where Hitler declared the unification of Austria and Germany, happened before the actual war started. Austria used that money from Germany to pay its reparations to the Russians, who insisted because the Austrians had been integrated into the German army. I think an awful lot of the soldiers who went into Russia were Austrians. Austria possibly had better ski trainers than Germany, but none of them were prepared for the kind of cold, and it was the cold that defeated them. But Austria had been taken, just like other overrun countries' armies had been absorbed into the German army.

The Austrians were always known to "change their coat with the wind," as the Austrian saying goes. They were ambivalent. They were going to vote as to whether or not they were going to join Germany, and so Germany marched into Austria instead. They marched right down the road along the Danube where we lived and went into the big *platz* there at the *hofburg* in Vienna. The pictures that you see of Hitler standing on the balcony, that's the big Winter Palace. And people walked to see him speak.

The main support the Nazis got from Austria, which we found when Ben was doing his research there, was that Austria was so poor and in such bad economic shape, and Austria began to see how there were jobs in Germany. It wasn't so much that they agreed with Hitler's politics. They didn't even know what his politics were. They just knew that he was charismatic, and people up there were working and able to feed their families. In Austria they were having lots of trouble doing that.

Anyway, Russia was the only country that insisted Austria pay them reparations, but Austria is also the only country that Russia withdrew from without a battle. When we were there, there was still a statue commemorating the Russian soldiers who had liberated the city from the Nazis in Vienna. And the deal was that if that statue were to have anything happen to it—if it was blown up, say—that the Russians would be entitled to come back in. So there was always an honor guard around it. I used to take Michael through that park and that plaza to his music lessons when he was small.

Michael took lessons from a music student there at the Academy who was from New Zealand. He lived in a little garret. We had to put a schilling in the elevator, which was all upholstered in red plush with crystal lights on the side, to ride up, but you couldn't ride the elevator down. You had to walk down. Then, from the elevator, we had to walk up two more flights of winding stairs to get to the student's garret. We would ride up the elevator, walk up two flights, and we would get to a room that was full of wooden bathtubs. Only thirty percent of the people in Vienna at that time had bathtubs, and when I saw that room, I said, "Now, I know where the other bathtubs are."

It was always nice and cold in the garret. There was always washing hanging on the line. Then there was another room that would be at least nominally heated. There was a grand piano in there and a little single bed. And a chair. And a desk. I would sit in the chair and face the desk instead of the piano while he and Michael had their lessons—not a lot of room in there, because that grand piano took up most of it.

Thinking back, that must have been an interesting expense, getting that grand piano into that garret, because I remember on our second visit getting a grand piano up into Mike's apartment that was up on the fifth floor. And I know they couldn't have gotten that grand piano in that elevator, so they had to walk it all the way up.

Michael's tutor told me to never be surprised if I got there and nobody answered the door because he was engaged to a Chinese girl who was the daughter of the Chinese diplomat in London, and her father was trying to take her back to China to marry somebody he had chosen. So he was trying to get away to London so that he could marry her, which he did. And we did get there one day and nobody answered the door, but there was no way he could have called me to let me know when he was gone.

The house we were living in sat on the corner of *Brahms-Gasse* and *Franz-Schubert-Gasse*, sort of appropriate names for living in Austria. "*Gasse*" just means "road" in German. *Brahms-Gasse* actually dead-ended into *Franz-Schubert-Gasse*, right beside a house owned by Dr. Tauber.

He lived in America at this point. Dr. Tauber had gotten out of Austria before the Second World War. His father, I think, was Jewish, and so he had been arrested. One of his aunts had turned him in and he was arrested at night. But his father had paid to get him out, and he had gotten out before Italy had closed its doors. So he had a passport to get out of Austria and then out through Italy to America. Somebody in America sponsored him.

Two old ladies lived there at Dr. Tauber's house our first visit. One of them was the aunt of Dr. Tauber. The other was the *hausfervalter*. The *hausfervalter* was somebody who lives in a sort of a separate part of your house and is something like a housekeeper. For instance, she will shovel your walk. If it snows in the middle of the night, someone must go out and clean the snow. That is what's expected. The sidewalk must be kept clear at all times. She would also do the shopping for the Dr. Tauber's aunt.

From time to time we would see them, and the old ladies sort of thought of our children as pets, particularly John, because he was the same age as Dr. Tauber's son. And I remember that when we left, they gave each child 20 schillings, and 20 schillings at that time for a child was like giving a ten-year-old $20 today would be. That was quite an amount of money for a kid to get.

When they gave him this money, John said, "We'll be back."

And the *hausfervalter* said, "Yes, but I am very old."

And John, bless his sweet heart, said, "Yes, you will probably be dead."

We went the first time to Austria for only a year and a half because ran out of money, and we had a house sitting back in Raleigh. Ben wanted to finish the book and not have to stop and write more paperbacks. He called those his "potboilers," and they did keep the pot boiling, as it were, in our kitchen. Also we didn't really want to become expatriates. We never got involved with the expatriate community in Austria. Ben always pointed out that we were just there to see how these people lived and to get a feel for their lives, and we have friends there that are still friends who we hear from, who visit back and forth, from this first visit that we were there.

Chapter Eight
If Johnson Had Sons

We came back on the United States line. We were scheduled to come back on an Italian ship, the Michelangelo, but it broke down just out of port before we were supposed to go, so we were transferred to the Raphael, and it caught fire. So then we re-booked. We were going out of Italy so we could see something of Italy, which Ben and I had never done before. This gave us the opportunity to visit friends of ours, Phyllis Riley— I called her "Sugar," Sugar Riley—and she married Gil Stevenson, who'd been an All-American for the Army.

They carried us to the train station in their two cars. One of them was on old Buick that, if you stopped it, the only way to get it started again was to push it down the hill—so much for the "rich Americans." Gil was driving that, and Sugar was driving their little VW. Suddenly we realized, after we had already gone through the passport check and said "goodbye" to them, that we had four boys instead of three, so he grabbed Gil and

Sugar's son Russ, who had just wandered along with my boys. We weren't sure whether both of them would have left, because each parent would have assumed that Russ was with the other.

Luckily, I think the Buick had stalled out, so we didn't end up having to bring Russ home with us. This was the same Russ Stephenson who was later elected to the Raleigh City Council.

We stayed in Paris several days. That was when Ben bit down on a piece of bread and said, "Damn, this stuff will break your teeth." And then he realized he just had. He actually broke his tooth on a piece of French bread.

We did not get a chance to eat in any of the fancy restaurants; you just do not take three little boys there. Our boys had done very well in Austria where people are very tolerant of children. In fact they thought our children were very well behaved. They had no idea American children were that well behaved, to say "Sir" and "Ma'am."

Of course we had not seen any black people for a long time, and the steward on the ship was black. Mr. President, John, walked over to the steward and said, "How do you do? My name is John Douglas Haas, and it sure is good to see a good American black man."

Luckily, he was a Southern black man. He picked John up and set him on his shoulders. Ben and I laughed. From that point on, our kids got entirely different treatment from the other kids. The ship was primarily being used to transport American military families back to the States, and so Ben and I had a state room and the boys had a big state room. And the steward would stick his head in and speak to them as if he were their parent, and say, "You boys get this room cleaned up before I send anybody in there to make the beds."

Vietnam was just heating up while we were in Austria. Ben was writing a column at the time for a little newspaper that some friends of ours were involved in getting out in Ohio. He wrote some about what his feelings then were about going into the war there, based on his experience with the Filipinos that he'd dealt with when he was in the military and stationed in the Philippines, that the average farmer there—and most of the people in Vietnam were farmers—weren't all that concerned about who the head of Vietnam was so long as he could make a living. And because of that, he thought we might end up there making more enemies than friends because we were interfering as we burned off land and encouraged fighting, making it harder for the general population to make a living.

Of course the Philippines was really the first major battle in the Pacific Theater after Pearl Harbor, but by the time Ben was there, the war was winding down, and so the farmers were trying to get back to the land. Because Ben had been the unit clerk, he was the last man out. He wrote his own papers to send himself home.

When we got back from Austria, I guess that's when we were protesting the war. Ben and I were less involved with the Vietnam protests partly because we were in Europe a good bit of the time. But certainly, as usual, Raleigh was probably more Liberal than the rest of the state in their view on that. Always, you've got a certain amount of conflict on it, but we knew an awful lot of guys who were the age for the draft, and that was a very big thing to talk about. I remember sitting up and watching them roll the numbers and being very relieved when Joel got a high number. I think that they were in the Capital Building. Whether they were in the Senate chamber or the House chamber, I don't remember. They said they used the same tub for turning that had been used for Bingo.

None of the kids we knew really intimately were drafted. They all stayed in college. I think there was one friend who did go to Canada, and I believe he stayed. I know that Charlie Ward was a conscientious objector and was certified as that, and his father, who had been the minister for the black Baptist church on Capital Square down here, had been a conscientious objector for the Second World War, which was very unusual.

There was an awful lot of talk about why did we think we could go in to Vietnam and do what the French, who had been there all this time, could not. Yet there was also an awful lot talked about the "Domino Theory," that if Vietnam fell to Communism the whole East would fall to Communism. Of course China already was.

The fathers of most of these guys had been in WWII, and many of them who'd seen combat didn't want to send their sons. Ben had the theory that if Johnson had sons instead of daughters, we might have been out sooner

More of the protests that were going on were with Civil Rights. The night that Martin Luther King, Jr. was shot, which of course was very early in the Civil Rights movement, I remember that people were told to stay in, stay off the streets. Ben was in Rex Hospital, the old Rex Hospital on St. Mary's Street. He'd had his first major heart attack, and so I went to go to the hospital to see him. It was interesting. I passed by the little back street there where the water tank is on Tower Street, kind of behind the banks on Oberlin Rd.

There is a playground there that, as long as I can remember, had a basketball court where black kids and white kids all shot hoops together. It's still there, and black kids and white kids still shoot hoops together. I pass by there frequently, going to the bank. That night, in spite of the fact that in the black section of town there were a couple of warehouses burned, the black kids and the white kids were still shooting hoops there. There may have been some riots in Durham, not on Oberlin Road, but I had too much else on my mind.

Joel, in the way of teenagers, rebelled, and he said he was the only friend he had whose parents were marching against the war. He was in high school at first, but then he was in college and he joined the Marines. This was a program they were running at the college. There was a recruiting officer who drove a little red convertible. The idea was that they could finish college, put in one summer of training, but any time before the training, they could resign.

By that time we knew that we were going back to Austria. Joel had moved to a little apartment across the street from us on Bedford, and he was going to stay behind. But when we left for Austria, the war really was heating up, and Joel realized that maybe his parents weren't all that crazy, so he went in and said he needed to help his parents get settled in their new world and resigned from the Marines.

We told our friends in Vienna that we wanted to come back and to watch for a place for us to live. Thanksgiving Day of 1972, Helmut Seif called and said that he had found a house in Klosterneuburg. Klosterneuburg has two parts, Kierling and Weidling, and this was in Weidling. He described the house, and it sounded good. Ben had another Book Club sale, so we knew we were ready to come back as soon as we could get some money together. He told Helmut that we would wire him money to go ahead and put a down-payment on the house, which Helmut did.

Michael and I went to Austria first. He had dropped out of high school and gotten his GED, but they wouldn't give him his certificate until he turned 18 in the fall. But it was obvious at that time that music was going to be Mike's life. We had talked about this at one time. Mike's also an excellent artist, and he said that painting and drawing came easier for him than music, but he knew he couldn't live a day without music, and by that time it was time to really concentrate on one or the other. He ended up going to the Conservatory in Vienna.

Her Words

There were all sorts of reasons for him dropping out. Mainly it was that he was disgusted because he was through with his classes by twelve o'clock, but he had to stay there until 3 PM. They wouldn't release him. At that time he was studying pipe organ at St. Mary's, and they wouldn't release him to go practice. He needed to practice an hour a day of pipe organ, plus at least an hour a day on the piano.

He had gone off to look at the Curtis Institute of Music in Philadelphia. I remember he stayed with my uncle and aunt. And the people at Curtis said, "You are already fluent in the language. Go back to Vienna." And that was what we all wanted to do anyway.

Michael did not really want to come back from Vienna after our first visit. He was really happy there. The other two I think enjoyed being there, but they did not resent coming back the way Michael did. I think part of that had to do with the fact that, as a boy interested in classical music, he was not considered an oddball there.

He particularly was a good friend of Werner Schiener, the son of Fritz and Friedl Schiener, whose house had been right beside ours. Werner wrote a wonderful letter to Michael about his father taking him up to the Czech border, to Gmünd, which was where we had crossed the border one spring when we went to Czechoslovakia. Fritz had taken Werner up to Gmünd to see the Czechs escaping from Czechoslovakia after the Prague Spring, which was a time when the Czechs took control of their own country and were very quickly stomped by the Russians. But during that time many Czechs crossed the border into the Austria at Gmünd, and there was a radio station, Free Czechoslovakia, that you could pick up there. So Werner wrote Mike about seeing them come through and hearing the radio station and all of this.

It was a wonderful letter. I said, "Michael, you should take this to school to your social studies class." He said he wouldn't do it, and I found out later it was because he and his social studies teacher had a big argument. Michael had stood up in class and said that Austria was not a Communist country, although his social studies teacher had insisted it was. But it wasn't.

So I took Mike and the dog and we flew to Vienna to set up the house and find a piano and a piano teacher for Mike. To get into the Academy in Europe, you find a major teacher first, and it's best if you find a major teacher who has more than a nodding acquaintance with the teachers there at the Academy. Our friends in Austria tracked down Panhoffer, who was the best teacher at the

Academy, and his former mistress was a Frau Bauenfein in Klosterneuburg, where we were going to live.

We found that John at fourteen was not entitled to public education unless he qualified for a music school or art school or something like that, but he had played first chair trumpet at Daniels Middle School in Raleigh. So three days after his trumpet arrived in Austria, he went for an audition. John has always had great stage presence. It made Mike madder than hell. He had been working like crazy all summer towards this audition, and John just walked in and aced it for trumpet.

I must say, it was interesting to hear the auditions. I could not go into the room when John was auditioning, but he was the youngest person I saw. There were people auditioning who had come from all over the world to get in to study trumpet there. I'm sure some of them weren't accepted, because I heard them blow it.

But that was as young as they would take a trumpet player. John studied with Helmut Voebish. Voebish was the first chair trumpeter and also the secretary of the orchestra, head man for the orchestra. They elect their head man; the first violinist isn't automatically it, as in other orchestras.

If Johnson Had Sons

So then John was eligible to go to the *musik gymnasium* once again. The *gymnasium* there is—or was at the time—the school used by Duke University for their junior year abroad classes, and John came home laughing one day because he said some girl had come up to him and in very halting German asked him where the principal's office was, and that he'd said, "Honey child, you just follow me!" And her expression, when he came out with this deep, deep Southern accent—I think that's one of his favorite memories there.

When John was in younger school, there were always kids from all over the world studying there. Some of them were diplomats' children as well as people like us or just students from just other parts of Europe. Anyway he said that in his class there was a girl who was I think English, and I don't know why she was there, but anyway he said that usually if they needed somebody to translate for an English visitor that she was chosen. But that one day he was chosen, and that he wasn't really sure why until he came out of the class and the teacher said, "We have a problem. The director of the British boys' choir, who is coming to join with our boys' choir here, is touring the school, and we don't know how to tell him that he hasn't closed his fly." John got to do the honors.

Her Words

Chapter Nine
The Un-Reconstructed Nazi

I looked at the house we found in Klosterneuburg and could see what was needed. One of the things we needed was a double bed. There weren't enough beds there.

Dora, who had been our baby-sitter before, when the kids were little, had married Helmut Seif. They had been good friends. So Dora and I went into a second-hand store called, appropriately, "The Chance." The name was actually a German word, but that name was so good for a second-hand store. I bought lots of things at either The Chance or the Dorotheum, which was this huge auction house where you can buy anything, from an old shoe to the crown jewels from some deposed emperor. I loved to just go in there and go through the place. It's not as much fun now as it used to be because they've sort of cleaned it up and you no longer find the old shoes thrown on some magnificent sofa somewhere.

At the Dorotheum, I never entered into the bidding part. They have one floor of things that had not met their minimum bid, and if you want to buy them, then you could take their number to one of the auctions, and they would make it so that you could bid right that minute, the minimum, and it was yours.

I got some household things—dishes, a mixer, ultimately a washing machine, a sewing machine, and skis for the kids. Helmut suggested that we get bicycles for the boys, so we got three bicycles for the summer too. I know we bought a radio and some lamps and all sorts of odds and ends that way. It was an inexpensive way to make the house more comfortable, more like what we would live in.

I remember the owner of the house, Herr Talner, was very upset that I had bought a double bed. The mattresses are very different there. They come in pieces, and there always was a sort of bundling board down the middle. We always figured that made for a good natural birth control in a Catholic country. Talner told me how unhealthy it was for people to share a bed. He never offered any explanation as to why. His mother' portrait, a full-length portrait of her sitting in a chair, hung over the only wall-space in the master bedroom big enough for a double bed, so I draped a sheet over it.

The Un-Reconstructed Nazi

Herr Talner had, as a military man during the Second World War, been in charge of interrogating English speaking flyers who were downed in Hungary, and I'm sure that those interrogations were not pleasant. So I knew that he knew how to speak English, but while he did not have authority to torture me, he could be very nasty in speaking. We decided he was the "un-reconstructed Nazi" from all the signs in the South about the "un-reconstructed rebels."

Helmut suggested that Talner never come to talk to me unless he was there to make sure that I understood everything that was said. I think Helmut didn't really trust him very much. He just didn't think Talner was maybe always on the up-and-up because one day, before Ben got there, Talner came by and demanded I pay him three-months' rent or something, and I wouldn't have it. I told him that, no, he was not to come over like that, and I couldn't discuss this without Herr Seif there also.

Ben needed an office, and so I began to ask around the neighborhood. I was told that perhaps Frau Velvert, who lived in the house up there on the hill, had a room she would rent. I walked over one afternoon, knocked on her door, and—in rather halting German—tried to explain that my husband was a *Schriftsteller*, a writer, and needed a *Büro*, an office.

She immediately changed into perfect English and said, "Oh, are you American?" She said, "Come on in! Have a cup of tea! Would you like some schnapps?"

Elizabeth Velvert became a very close friend of ours. She had been married three times. Her third husband had been an American, but she had never lived in the States. She had studied English.

Her father was a monarchist and an officer in the Foreign Service. The monarchists were against both the republic that had been set up in Austria after WWI, after Franz Josef abdicated, and also against the Nazis. They wanted one of the Hapsburgs to return. And her father had the moustache that Franz Josef had.

She did have a room she could rent to Ben upstairs. It was a very nice room, and the only thing in it that was made after 1600 was Ben's typewriter. There were little hand-carved cherubs around the wall and beautiful old farmer furniture in there as well as a more elegant bed. There was indoor plumbing. In fact, there were several stories to this house. Eventually this house became the model for the house Ben used in *The House of Christina*, because on the back of this particular house, it was written "The House of Elizabeth."

Ben used to tell about going to the bathroom—it was an American bathroom because it had the toilet and tub all in one room instead of having the toilet separate—and finding this big, wooden Madonna soaking in the bathtub in some sort of preservative. Elizabeth had a daughter who had studied at the school for preserving antiquities and was married to another preservationist. In the summer, they lived down in the country, where we were, and in the winter time they sold antiques and lived and worked in an apartment in the city.

The House of Christina was the last major novel he ever wrote, and it was the only one that was never translated into German. It was very popular, but his editor and his agent said that the publisher that had always done his books in German felt like, at the time it came out, in 1977, the German-speaking public was not willing to accept the picture of Hitler as Ben had portrayed him, in Hitler's years when he was a student in Vienna. Oddly enough, what this was based on was one day we had gone to Baden. That's where John found that the urinals in the men's room there in the park had different tones on their electric eye, so he had this idea of playing the

Anvil Chorus by peeing in different ones. Unfortunately, I could not go into the men's room and hear this, but Ben went—an experience he never thought he'd have.

Anyway, we were coming back from Baden, and we passed by a big book sale being put on by the Austrian Lions Club, just as here, raising money for the blind. Ben was not able to pass a book sale, a used book sale particularly, but also often at places like that we got copies of books that had been forbidden and been burned by the Nazis. One of the things that he got there at Baden was a book that had been ordered by the American Army, by their psychological division. They had interviewed people who had known Hitler. When the Americans withdrew, they left their library just out on the street because we had friends who had a lot of children's books in English. It was not a bound book. It was one of these things like a theme paper in a folder with the prongs holding it. I wish I knew what happened to it.

But in all the interviews, the two things I do remember from them were the piercing blue eyes Hitler had and what a charismatic person he was. The other thing though was they talked about what he had done to support himself. He had posed for pornographic postcards. So the whole point of the premise in *The House of Christina* was a man who was trying to find the woman who had posed with Hitler, so that he would have proof of what went on. There may have been some controversy about that had Ben not died just as *The House of Christina* was coming out.

When John would go into school every morning, there was a nurse, Frau Hutta, who lived in the house two doors up from us. She would drive down to Klosterneuburg. So he would go and clean her car of snow every morning, and she would give him a ride down to where he could take the train in, a quicker trip to the center of the city than if he had to start in Kritzendorf where we lived.

One night she came by to tell John that she wasn't going into work in the morning, so he would have to catch the train down in Kritzendorf, and there was a book out on the table that Ben was using to research *The House of Christina*. The cover had a big Nazi emblem on it with all these people walking by, and as Frau Hutta walked in, she saw it. She picked it up and said, "Ah, those were the days. Of course, I was the last person to join the party, but I had to join to keep my job at the hospital." We used to laugh at the people who told us they were the last people to join the party. There must have been a line that would have reached around the world with the "last" people who joined the party.

One day, there was a mudslide while I was out of the house, and the mud came all into the basement of the house we were renting from Herr Talner. John and Mike and Michael's best friend Larry Bliss who had come to visit were all helping Herr Talner shovel the mud out. He promised the boys he was going to pay them for the work, but he never did. In the course of shoveling, they found Talner's old Nazi membership and pictures of him in uniform and whatnot, and he found the boys going through his Nazi papers. He got very upset about that.

After that, Talner started coming constantly on weekends to do one thing or another at the house and to see whether we were looking after his possessions. Four boys, sometimes five boys, were living there that summer, and a dog. Larry Bliss was staying with us and David, the son of my uncle Doug, who was a sort of outlaw kin. So Herr Talner knew there were all of these teenage boys. What would they break?

He had been an officer and officers in the army *dutz* one another. There is a formal way of speaking in German, and there is an informal way. To *dutz* means that you speak informally. You're friends of theirs. If you were all the pupils of the same teacher—you all studied with Liszt, maybe—you *dutz*-ed each other. If you studied with someone who studied with Liszt, you *dutz*-ed too. It's a very formal idea of who *dutz*-es and who doesn't *dutz*.

You just knew this in the same way that there are barriers in the South between blacks and whites, that it was the way things were done. Children in Austria until about my generation did not *dutz* with their parents, just as in Southern children, my generation and my sons' generation were taught to say "sir" and "ma'am."

Anyway, I was complaining to Elizabeth about Talner, and she said, "Oh, I know who he is. We'll fix him." He evidently did not have the proper ancestry to be an officer in the Emperor's army, just the Nazi Army. Elizabeth said, "Yes, I remember him. I met him at a funeral. He came and spoke to my father, and my father did not answer. He introduced himself again, and my father said, 'Yes, I know you.'" But when he said, "I know you," he did not *dutz*, which was like being slapped in the face.

So, I said to Herr Talner, "I'm having guests over next weekend, and I'd appreciate it if you did not come to call. We'll be having tea on the terrace." It was a lovely place to have tea, and he did have some lovely dishes and glasses. We had rented the place furnished, after all. So we set the table out there on the terrace with all the best crystal and linen and that sort of thing. Elizabeth went by her house, and one of her son's friends was a very presentable young man with a car, which was a very unusual thing. Most of them didn't have cars there.

Talner did come over, and he stripped down to his underwear to go out and paint. He regularly painted in his underwear, in his shorts. He did have on shoes. And out came Elizabeth, striding in as only Elizabeth could do, as the grand duchess, and she had this young man with her who was in his twenties. As I recall, he was wearing an ascot. Elizabeth introduced him as Count Somebody-Or-Other.

And I said to Herr Talner, "Oh, I presume you know my friend Frau Velvert." He knew immediately who this was. He tried to click his heels. Have you ever seen a man try to click his heels in his underwear?

And Talner said, "Excuse me, Madame." She offered her hand, and he tried to kiss it. He was trying so desperately.

So we all went out on the terrace, and there were cucumber sandwiches and wine. Joel wasn't yet there, but Mike and John and Larry Bliss were there, and Elizabeth and Count Whoever, and we were all sitting around. The boys were showing off their German, which they'd learned. And I casually said, "Oh, Herr Talner, would you like a glass of wine?"

Larry went back, and he got another glass. He got one of Talner's good glasses. And I said, "Oh, Larry, I'm sure Herr Talner doesn't want us using one of his good glasses. I think there's one of those mustard glasses on the sink."

Mustard at that time was sold in what were called "Roman glasses," which were little round, stemmed glasses, so that, just like jelly glasses here, they became your everyday drinking glasses—and of course they were marked to where they could be filled. Every glass in Austria must have that mark on it, because a farmer may use that glass to sell his own wine, and therefore you have to know that you are getting what you paid for, which is supposed to be an eighth of a liter. If the wine doesn't come up to that little mark on the glass, it's a *schwindel*.

We did not give Herr Talner a *schwindel*, but we did give him wine in a mustard glass. Of course we were using the good glasses, so I had treated him as just a workman and not the owner. He did not come back for a number of Saturdays after that, and when he did, it was with a great deal

149

more of respect, but we were already looking for another place.

Long after we had moved out, Talner discovered all the skinned hares Ben had shot while we were there, because we left them. We forgot them. We forgot they were curing in the basement.

We heard that the old ladies who lived in Dr. Tauber's house had, in fact, died, so we contacted him in the United States to see what was the status of the house after we found out from the Schieners that nobody was living there. The Taubers had come and spent a year there after their aunt had died, but they didn't know what was going to be done apart from that.

Dr. Tauber that he wasn't sure about the condition of the house. He said the Schieners had the key, so I went to Friedl and I said, "We want to go to the house."

And she said, "Oh, sure. Come on, I have a key for the back door." We went to the back door, which was the kitchen, and there on the counter was a wooden box all filled with keys, thirty-some, as I recall. Only some of the keys said what they were, and every door in the house was locked. John and I had gone that day. So we went around, trying all the keys. It became like a Marx Brothers thing, the three of us going from room to room, trying to figure out which key went to which room. All of the rooms opened off from each other. They didn't open from a central hall. Also every drawer was locked, and there weren't any closets. There were these big wardrobes, and those were all locked. The keys were all in this box. There was no master key. Everything had its own key, and these wardrobes, many of them blocked the windows. When we finally opened them, there were clothes inside that had rotted along the edges, they had been folded so long.

We were told that, if we would see to doing some modernization of this house, that we could rent it for $200 a month. It took us several months to make it livable, to get the wardrobes moved to the attic, to empty the living room and the dining room. I have a picture of me standing in the front yard of the house with a pear tree, and beside me is the third floor of our neighbors the Schiener's house—that's how steep the lots were. The house had a huge yard, about an acre full of fruit trees, because the Taubers had a little fruit store in Vienna.

When Dr. Tauber and his family had come to stay there that year—I guess it was his sabbatical—they had put in a toilet on the main floor and a little lavatory. We would call it a "half-bath." In many, many houses that were there, the bathtub was in the kitchen. It was sort of half-walled-off to the side, and there was a sort of heater that warmed up the water as you were using it. I don't know why we don't use more of those here. For the bathtub, it would maintain a tank of water, but when I would wash dishes, I had another little heater under the sink, and I turned on the hot water for that.

They did put in a toilet downstairs, but they didn't run the waterline to it, although the waterline went to the room right next door to it because that was where all the washing was done. You had to fill a bucket and keep the bucket in the toilet, so you could use that to flush the toilet, but the toilet was connected to a septic tank outside, and when the *sinkgruber* would come—he's the man who empties your septic tank—you wouldn't want this strange man walking around in your yard or having the gate open, so there was a little tiny opening in the gate that was just the right size from him to put the hose through to your septic tank. Everybody's house was set up like that.

We hired some people to repaint. Another friend had a brother who was an electrician, and he came and did some wiring for us and put in an electric stove in the kitchen. I bought it from the electric company, and it was like the old stove that we'd had when Michael was a baby. It had flat panels that were very hard to control the heat on and a little tiny oven and a little tiny refrigerator.

It wasn't a year-round home, so there wasn't any heat in it, only one of those old coke stoves. These are the kinds of stoves you see in palaces. This was one that you used in the home, but you see pictures of them in palaces. You don't see where anybody could put coal in it, and it was ceramic, white, with angels on it maybe, or eagles or whatever. And because the walls are all so thick, if you have a coke fire, they're fed from the back. There are little halls in the back that had the place where you could put coal in. But the ones at home often had a spot inside the room where you could put the coke in and take the ashes out from. It gave a wonderful heat. Of course the walls, even the interior walls, would be twelve-inches thick, and overnight the walls will have heated, and you would open the windows and air the room out in the morning first thing, which everybody did. They were these double-paned windows. You close those in about fifteen minutes and feel comfortable again. Ben's English publisher had said to him, "Oh, I envy you, going to Austria. They know how to survive in the winter."

Her Words

We decided not to use the coke stove, because we had no idea how to control it, and I was told to go to see Rachman Ferrer. He was the chimney sweep, but he was also a heating engineer and could tell me what I needed to heat the house. So I went down to the heating store, and at the heating store this chubby man came and greeted me in English with a Brooklyn accent. He was Ferdinand Karp. He said, "Ferdinand, like the bull. And Karp, like the fish." When the Americans set up their housing for their occupation families in Salzburg, he had become the heating engineer for them. That was where he had honed his English, and he had picked up a Brooklyn accent.

At the age when music students went to the *music gymnasium*, other Austrians will go to a *hauptschule* and they may work half the day. If you were going to be a banker, you would work in a bank half a day and you would study things related to banking half a day. They don't look towards college in quite the same way that we do. To have gotten your Matura is the only way you may actually then get into a university, and that is quite a thing. Normally a heating engineer would not have been a man who had his Matura. But Ferdinand did, and it gives a sort of social status.

The Un-Reconstructed Nazi

Ferdinand became a sort of adjunct member of the family. He came out and told us what sort of oil stove to buy and that the boys should build a kind of brick thing inside the little glassed-in porch downstairs, so I could put a little can in it and fill it with oil and take it upstairs to the stove.

We had been there for three months when we found another room. Friedl said she thought that area was just the stairs to the *dachboden*, which is an attic. Turned out it was a key to where absolutely gorgeous China was stored. And we'd been there a year when Frau Kainrat, the maid who'd come to work for me, was trying to find a place to dry clothes, because there were no clothes dryers. She was cleaning out the shed behind the house that was next to the little cook's house. John lived in the cook's house. It was connected to the kitchen by a glass enclosure. Anyway, she came in laughing like crazy and said, "You got to come and look."

I went out to look, and there was a toilet in that shed that we had never known was there. So much stuff had been piled on top of it!

Of course, all of the bathroom fixtures in the house had been taken out and buried when the Russians came into that zone, because they were shooting anybody who had an indoor toilet. The

Russians figured that meant they were the bourgeoisie.

And I said, "I understand all of this perfectly; the silver was buried in the garden."

Chapter Ten
The Yugolenia Line

We lived in Austria for three and a half years that time, and toward the end of our stay, we had a big party at our house celebrating Mike's eighteenth birthday. The tradition in Austria is that there is a big party for an eighteenth birthday. The family buys a keg. I remember Ben, when he tapped the keg, he didn't get it in there tight enough to begin with, and it shot out of there and knocked him over backwards and just drenched him in beer.

The boys had their friends there, and we had some friends there too. They don't separate the adults from the children the way we do. It was like a Mungering. The Mungers used to have these big New Year's parties, and as the children got older, there would be teenagers, college kids, professors, and friends. There were people there from sixteen to ninety, everybody celebrating together, and this was the same thing that these parties were like.

I remember commenting that I supposed the reason we saw so few kids drunk was that their parents were there. And Ben said, "Yeah, you might notice that you don't see that many parents drunk because their kids are here too."

The evening of the party, we heard on the English-language radio that the draft had been abolished in the United States, so the it became a great celebration the Mike did not have to go and register and did not stand in any danger of being drafted.

It snowed like crazy. Even for Austria it was more than they would try to go home in. I remember there was a bunch of kids who ended up staying the night, and I ran out of food. I don't remember what I did—probably went and knocked on the door of the restaurant down the street.222

By that time, Mike had been living for some time in an apartment in Vienna off *Mariahilferstraße* in the upstairs of an old building that had been built in the 1500s. Another music student had been living there, and they swore the place was haunted. Then he moved to an apartment that was really a fairly nice little place in the second district, which had been the Jewish district, on the other side of the Danube canal.

That's where I convinced the piano movers to walk up five flights of stairs carrying a grand piano because it wouldn't go in the elevator, and the stairs twisted around the elevator. We'd had a friend in the military who would go to Germany to the PX and they would bring us things. I asked her to bring us a carton of cigarettes, so I gave the movers a carton of cigarettes. Two guys carried it all five flights, with a sling between them to hold the piano. They were both huge men. They took the legs off the piano, put the piano in the sling, and a third man carried the stool. I had always heard that the third man in piano moving carried the stool, and he really did. He also helped keep the piano from tipping as they went around these stairs. Now, how Michael got it out, I don't know, because we left before he did. That was his problem.

That time we came back to the United States on the Yugolenia line, which was a freighter line run by the Yugoslavian government. We had a friend, Gloria, who was a Hungarian. Oddly enough, she had a degree in costume design from the University of Maryland. She and I became good friends, as you can imagine. She told me that she and her parents had escaped and were living in Maryland. Apparently there was sort of a colony of Austrians living in Maryland.

Anyway, Gloria told us that they always travelled either on the Yugoslavian line or the

Polish freighters. So we went to Thomas Cook, and had Thomas Cook book us, and they booked us out of Yugoslavia on the Yugolenia line.

When you travel by freighter, you're never sure exactly when you're going to leave, but they were obligated, since we had been booked through Thomas Cook, to let us know three days before sailing. I had packed and was ready for us to go. The only things we had were just suitcases that we were living out of as it came close to the time for us to leave. These trunks had crowns painted on them. In fact some of them had brass plates too, and the crown would have nine balls on it, which meant that they had belonged to a baron.

So we got to Yugoslavia, to Rijeka, where we were to sail. We went into the office of the Yugolenia line, and they said, "You're here too early."

And Ben handed them the letter, telling us we were to come. They stood there with their thumb over the thing that says, "You will appear on such and such a date," pretending it wasn't there. Ben picked the paper up and pointed it out, and said he wanted the tickets now.

And they said, "You'll have to come back tomorrow because we have something in our typewriter today." They had only one typewriter in the office. This was in 1975.

The Yugolenia Line

We ended up being there three weeks, just Ben and me, a thousand pounds of luggage, and our border collie named Lady. And because Thomas Cook had told us to get there so early, they ended up having to put us up in a hotel and feed us for three weeks, us and also a lot of retired people from Florida. It was a big thing then to sail out of Florida on a freighter and you made stops all along the way. It was a lot of fun. It was a long trip, but if you've got a lot of time, it's a cheap way of seeing a lot of the world.

They kept saying, "We're going to sail in three days," and so none of us got any more money into the country. We had come down with enough money just to last us. We didn't want to have to change any more money into Yugoslavian money, not knowing what it would end up being worth.

I must say it was very nice in Rijeka, but there wasn't that much to do. We had a balcony that looked over the Adriatic. I could look straight down into the water. They don't have beaches like we do. There were all rocks, so we would go down to bottom of the hotel and swim.

We didn't have any children with us. You know, Robert Benchley used to say there are two classes of travel, first class and "with children." I want to tell him there's another class, and that's "with dog." Lady had to be walked because she refused to relieve herself anywhere unless it was grassy. Well, this meant at night you were out walking, and at that time there was such a shortage of housing in Yugoslavia. Young couples who got married might be living with the family where there were three or four couples as well, so the only way to have any privacy might be to go to the park in the shadows. So I had to be very careful that the dog was not uphill from any of these people enjoying a little privacy in the park at night.

Ben had a book that he wanted to finish, so after it was obvious that we were going to be there long, I talked to the purser and he helped me unpack the trunk that I knew that the typewriter was in. In fact, it was the trunk that I had the book put at the top of, and Ben had to go to the warehouse and get that box. It's very hard to get stuff like that moved in a country where there is no advertising for services, because they all were Communist. The only way you do it is you find the right palms to grease.

So there Ben was with the purser, unpacking this box, and he had to prove that it belonged to us. He opened the box. Our name with our address had been painted on the top of the thing, and there was Ben's book, a copy of *Look Away, Look Away*.

It just happened to have been turned to where his picture showed.

And the guy looked at him and said, "You write?"

And Ben said, "Yes."

And he said, "You give me?"

It was one of the copies that I think Ben had written in for one of the children, but he said, "Yes."

And he said, "Have brother in America. I'll read." Then he just closed the box. He didn't go through it, which Ben thought he was going to do. The box was taken down to the pier by some means. I guess he helped Ben find a truck to get it there.

So we got Ben's typewriter. Ben realized his typewriter had dried out and he needed carbon paper, so that he always had a copy of whatever it was he was typing. Most writers used to do this, before there were computers. So he sent Lady and me downtown to get some. You can take dogs everywhere in Europe. That's when I realized how much dogs understand.

She never responded to the people who spoke any sort of Slavic language to her, but she responded very quickly after we'd been there a short time—sort of like children learning—to the people speaking German with her. We had lived right there where the ladies who would come up shopping would stop at my fence, because some went down *Brahms-Gasse* and some went on up *Franz-Schubert-Gasse*, and they would stop there and talk. And Lady would sit there at the corner as if she were involved in the conversation too. They used to laugh about it. Of course they often brought her scraps that they had begged off the butcher.

Anyway, I went in Rijeka with just my German and almost non-existent Spanish, which wouldn't do me any good there, and did find typewriter ribbon. I had taken a typewriter ribbon with me to make sure I got the right size. Then I had to explain that I wanted carbon paper, and I got a box of carbon paper.

I got back, and this is where Ben is lucky he didn't die right there, because as I gave it to him he said, "But you bought me pencil carbon, not typing carbon."

And I said, after a few choice words, "If you want carbon paper, you go buy it yourself!" I've always felt that was the height of my making myself understood in a foreign country, finding carbon paper in Rijeka, Yugoslavia.

Finally, the boat was ready and we did depart from Rijeka. We stopped at various places. Probably the most interesting thing that happened, which I'm sure that Ben would have eventually worked into a book, was that we stopped in Lisbon and they were having a revolution there. So we and the couple from Richmond hired a taxi driver to take us around to see what was going on.

I don't really know how dangerous it was. We didn't speak enough Portuguese, but I decided, when you have revolutions like that, he who has the most red spray paint wins. The people who lived in the fancy houses there, most of them had left. We did not stay in Lisbon as long as we thought we were going to, but one of the things that we did take on from there was a couple and their two little boys. She was an American married to a Portuguese man, and with their children they had been living in Portugal, evidently very well. They had walked out of their home, where they had servants, and did not say any more than that they were just leaving to take the children to school or whatever that morning. Then they drove to the pier and found this ship, which was the Yugolenia, and bought passage and had their Mercedes hoisted on board. They had no change of clothes or anything. I remember feeling choked-up for her when we got off the ship at Brooklyn in the freight harbor because they made her throw out her African violet that she had brought with her. It was understandable why they did, but she said it was the only thing she had from home.

And I cried that time when I saw the Statue of Liberty. I remember people trying to get their cars started while we were trying to look for one to rent that would be big enough for the four of us and the dog and the trunks. Ben's driver's license had expired while he was gone, so he couldn't drive. The woman in the couple from Virginia had lost her glasses, and so she couldn't drive. So her husband and I ended up driving.

Like I said, none of us had gotten any more money in before we left Europe and arrived on the weekend. The banks were closed. We couldn't do anything. So it was just what we had between us. We put three dollars of gas into the car because that was all that we had, and it got us just into their driveway.

Chapter Eleven
Raleigh Creative Costumes

I loved living in Europe, and I still love to visit, but I particularly loved being there at that time because women were never asked, "What does your husband do?" and that was a phrase that used to really rankle me. "What does your husband do?" That never assumed that you might do something yourself. In Austria it was assumed that, if you were at this gathering, you were there because of being of interest to somebody, and not just because you were attached to someone interesting.

We got home to Raleigh and found that our house had been rented to a bunch of hippies, that it had been turned into a drug house. They'd pretty much destroyed what was there. Luckily, we had put the grand piano at my parents. The dining room table legs had been broken, but that was reparable. The sideboard, I'm sure that it lost a lot of value, because one of the panels off the top was broken and couldn't be repaired, and one of the posts just had to be reconstructed. And there was no living room furniture that was usable.

John had spent the night there before we returned, and he got to see the tenants. He said they raised puppies on the sun porch and the place was so overrun with fleas that he slept in a sleeping bag with flea collars on his ankles and wrists. We had to have the house exterminated. So that house was where Raleigh Creative Costumes was started because there was nothing else left in it.

I found that theater had expanded in Raleigh. Ira David Wood III had started Theater in the Park, and a lot of people had left Raleigh Little Theater to follow him. Thompson Theater at NC State University had begun to put on plays for the public. I remember costuming a couple plays over there later on. State was just then going from being an engineering school to having a liberal arts department. They still don't have a drama department. It's all done out of the Department of Communication.

And Wat kept being involved with theater even after there weren't as many parts open for an older character actor, but she began to do stuff in Wilmington for the movies. She still had an Equity card from New York. But Wat never went to the "cattle calls." She only went if she knew it was something where she was going to have lines.

She loved the story that John told about how, when he went to California, he saw the movie *Reuben, Reuben*, and it opens with Wat's face filling the screen. He called her afterward and said, "I was so excited that I threw up my hands, forgetting that I had a big thing of popcorn, and rained popcorn all over the people who were close by."

Sue Scarborough I met when I was working at RLT for John Miller and Harry Callahan. Sue came down and was in a play, *The Man with the Golden Arm*, I believe, and that was where she met Tony, her future husband and future ex-husband. Tony was one of the characters then in *A Funny Thing Happened on the Way to the Forum*… This was the production that the big RLT theater fight surrounded, and Guy Mungers covers that nicely in his book, *Curtain Up!*

But I liked Sue, and then when Harry left RLT, he went to work at St. Mary's, where they promised him they were going to build a nice theater. They never have. They still are using the same inadequate theater space, but Sue became his costumer there.

So when Ben and I came back from Europe in '75, in September, I called Sue and I said, "What is going on with theater costuming here?"

And she said, "Well, it's just like it's always been. They rent something from Brooks van Horne in New York, maybe one or two costumes, and then pay a pittance to have somebody here make all the rest of them."

And I said, "You know, Sue, you and I could rent them those extra costumes."

Ron Campbell was directing at that time at RLT and was doing *George M.* with Joel Adams playing the lead, and Martha Christian, who was doing costumes for him, had done her first costume under me. Later, Martha left and went to the Barter Theater. Actually the Costumer's Handbook, the cover of it, has costumes that Martha did.

Martha called, knowing I was back in town, and said, "Doug, could you make a set of white satin tails for Joel?" And I said yes. So I went down, took my sewing machine and made the white satin tails.

Well, the word had gotten out that Sue and I were thinking about renting some costumes, and it was Halloween week. Martha and I had cleaned up the costume room down at the theater and were bringing my sewing machine home. Ben was standing on the steps when I got there and said, "I cannot work here with the phone ringing like this all the time, people wanting to rent costumes. I've called Charlotte and there is a man there who has a costume shop who will rent you some costumes at thirty percent off, and you can bring them here and rent them out and bring them back him after Halloween." This was Morris, who even then had a fairly good-sized shop in Charlotte. So we started taking orders from people for what they wanted for Halloween.

Sue had a little Pinto. She couldn't stop working on *The King and I* right then to help with the sewing, but we drove to Charlotte and filled that Pinto up. I had ordered curtains to go in the living room of our house. We'd had to have the living room and dining room re-wall-papered and painted. The new curtains were the wrong length but there were ladders up in both rooms where I'd been putting the curtains up, and so we hung costumes that we had gotten from Charlotte on those ladders.

After getting things that people had said they wanted, we then picked up just a few other things that we thought we might rent, and we called all of our friends and said, "If you have a costume, we will rent it and give you a third, and we will see that it's being mended and cleaned." And we kept the rest.

Ben put up seventy-five dollars and Tony put up seventy-five dollars. When Sue and I first went to a bank to talk to them about borrowing some money to set up a costume shop, they didn't consider that a business. They thought we were two women out of our heads. And maybe we were.

We used the money we had then to buy some fabric, and we made things that we knew we would use again. We made, I remember, two witch costumes and witch hats--and swore we'd never make witch hats again--and a huge cape. But most everything was stuff that we'd got ready-made, and we charged people about $10 a piece. I remember the last thing we rented out Halloween night was Guy Munger's tuxedo. We put a cape on it and sent a man out as Dracula. I don't know why he rented it when he could use his own tuxedo, surely.

We didn't have a cash register, and of course there weren't charge cards then. The first day that Sue and I realized we had taken in a thousand dollars in cash, we were so excited that we locked the door and we threw the money up in the air and were rolling on the floor. We didn't realize there was a customer still in one of the bathrooms.

Raleigh Creative Costumes

That Halloween, we made enough that we paid Martha and paid to have a telephone line put in in downstairs of Sue's house. She and Tony were living over on Barmettler Street in a house that had belonged to her parents. It was on a sloping lot and the downstairs was finished, but they weren't really using it. There were two bedrooms and a bath and a rec room, so we just took that space over. And Tony built some racks and Ben wrote some letters for us. We got a rubber stamp to stamp stationery. Rubie's Costume Company was the first place to acknowledge that we were a real business and should have a wholesale catalog. We did make Santa Claus suits and what we needed was a beard and wig set, so we called Ruby's.

The first show we did was for the Neuse Little Theater and it was *Oklahoma!*, which is a great show to have as your first. I still used some of those over twenty years later because the dresses and the men's bright coats are all good for so many plays that use those sort of country or old-fashioned clothes. We bought at thrift shops some plaid jackets and piped them all around with bright colors to make them show up better on stage.

I think Martha Christian had a few costumes that she donated. One of them was a red suit that you can make into a bustle suit for a woman. I think she made it in the Old Barn Dinner Theater. And, as I said, a few friends donated some. Then as time went on, we began to buy some of these things from our friends.

I never bought Wat's things. I just kept paying her for their use. By that time, she was beginning to always be a little short of money, and this was one way that there was always a little bit of money coming in from some rental. I had made a lot of her costumes, of course, but she also had just some beautiful clothes that we could rent.

Ben was working hard trying to finish *The House of Christina*, plus writing Westerns and a few suspense novels and a couple fantasies. Sometimes Joel would write some of the Westerns. Ben had just sent off the manuscript for *The House of Christina*, and the next day he had a massive heart attack and was hospitalized.

When we got back from Austria, we found out our doctor had closed his practice and so I had gone looking for a new one. And when I found a doctor I liked, I said, "You're probably going to meet my husband in the Emergency Room, having a heart attack," and that was true.

Ben had destroyed about a quarter of his heart, so he was much restricted in his physical doings afterward. He got to where he couldn't walk but a mile a day and he was exhausted from it. He did not recover in the way he had from his first heart attack.

I said, "I'll quit this costume shop. You're going to need somebody at home."

But he said, "You're going to need something to do," which I think was prophetic. I think he realized that he couldn't go on like this. That winter he said, "I don't want to live if I have to live like this anymore."

The next Halloween, this Literary Guild was having this big party for its authors in New York, and since he'd had several books that were Literary Guild selections, he was one of their prize authors at that time. So he went up for that.

He wanted to see his agent, and he wanted to see his publisher and talk about the next book he wanted to do. He had it outlined. And he wanted to do this dinner. Normally he would try to do it all and just stay up one night, but his doctor said, "If you go, just do one of these things each day."

So he went by himself. Mary Munger was in New York at the time, and she had left an Old South dress at the costume shop at one time that had been a part of our collection. She called and said, "I would love to go as a Southern Belle to a party up here. Could Ben bring my costume?"

I said, "Sure," and I packed up the hoop and the dress with Ben's stuff

That afternoon Mary called him and said, "Come down and have a drink with me and my boyfriend."

And Ben said, "I'm tired. I think I'm going to have a nap, and I'll just leave your dress and the hoop at the desk." He had always stayed at the Algonquin, but the Algonquin had been full because of this Literary Guild party, and he'd been late making reservations, so he stayed across the street. The maid found him dead there the next day.

Wat was doing a show at The Village Dinner Theater, and she said she was driving home and heard it on the radio. Joel and his first wife had just gotten married. They got married in the First Baptist Church, and the minister there said he heard it on the radio too. So these were the first two people who appeared at my house—strange combination.

Somebody was going to have to go to New York and identify him. So Mary Munger and her Jewish lawyer friend went. She was playing in a Broadway show at the time, so she was up late. The next morning she was in what my children used to call a "foreign correspondents rain coat" with dark glasses and a lawyer. And she said that

176

all the newspaper men were there because they had heard that Jimmy Hoffa had been found and they thought they had pulled Jimmy Hoffa's body out. Ben would have just loved this. She told me years later, they all thought she was Jimmy Hoffa's girlfriend being brought in by his lawyer. Mary went in and she said that she had seen Ben the afternoon before and identified him. They released his body and they shipped him to Raleigh.

He had just turned 51. This was 1977. The funeral was on Halloween day.

John was in Chapel Hill at the time. Michael was still living in Europe, in Vienna. Joel's first wife, Jeanie, her mother had been a telephone operator, and this was a time when her connections came in handy because at that time, in Austria, that was the beginning of one of their major holidays, All Saints.

We had just gotten a letter from Michael, saying that was going to marry this girl, Leslie, and she worked at St. Ninian's where he hoped to be hired as music director. I knew of no way to get in touch with him. The only thing I did know was that he had gotten a job at a big record store that was in the Haas building that was across from *Stephansplatz*, which is in the middle of Vienna, but Jeanie's mother knew a German-speaking

177

telephone operator and called her and said, "We've got to get in touch with this guy before everything closes down so he can get cash from friends to buy a ticket to get home." And she did.

I had to call and tell him on the telephone at work that his father had died and gave him the option to come home or stay there.

And he said, "Of course I'm coming home."

My father went out and bought a plot at the old cemetery there in Goldsboro, because he said that he had seen too many people have to go and see to this in a crisis time. So this was for four people. My parents are buried there, Ben is buried there, and I will be buried there in Willowdale Cemetery.

Joel did some lovely abstract dancing angels cast in bronze that he had mounted on stone that each space has a different angel. Somebody stole one and one came off. The other two were there last time I was there.

Oddly enough, paperwork takes forever it looks like, because we were all sitting on the porch after his burial in Goldsboro after supper. The police came to the door, so the boys went to see what it was all about. They said that they had a body in New York. "You need to go and identify your father's body."

And Joel said, "You mean we have to dig him up?"

Michael stayed about three months. He got a job at NC&B. They wanted him to stay in on their training program, and he said, "You know, Mom, I hate to leave you here."

And I said, "Look, I didn't get all those pianos moved for you to stay here and go into banking. Go back to Vienna." So that's what he did.

I didn't take any time away from the costume shop. That was my salvation, because when you come in to the shop, nobody knows if you've got troubles, and coming there gets your mind off the troubles. It's very hard to have people always giving you their sympathy. It's very nice, but it's also very hard to respond.

I found it much easier if I brought up the subject of Ben. Even today, I find that, whether it's Ben or Willard. If I bring up the subject, it's easier than if somebody else does.

Chapter Twelve
How Long Do You Cook Potatoes?

Sue and I knew that we needed more space for Halloween, and that's when we began to shop around and found a little house on West Johnson Street that's since been torn down. It was an interesting little house. It was too big for us to begin with, and it had an enclosed porch with a door that opened outside. The window that would have gone onto that porch had been blocked up, and we rented that to a man who billed himself as a "divorcement counselor." He misspelled "divorcement" on the sign.

To begin with, Sue and I thought this would be something that would be just a winter time business, that we wouldn't have much to do in the summer. The summer after Ben died, I went to Europe. Sue didn't think there would be enough going on for it to really take much of her time. She would just take phone calls at home and run down if someone wanted to make an appointment, but when I got back she said, "Doug, you know, I've still got a small child, and I really can't have my summers like this." So I bought Sue out. We didn't have a fight or anything and split. It was just that I had time and I had a little bit of money.

I hired Ruth Bicket to help. Ruth had done a bit of sewing for us. She'd made a few petticoats. And Shoshanna Serxner, whose son David later came to work for me too, had set up the original books for us. She went down with me to Goldsboro one weekend, and she and my father set up the books—well, my father and mother. I guess it was really my mother who was the main bookkeeper, but my father's handwriting was on all of it. Of course, this was before computers.

Shoshanna said, "Doug, you really need somebody who is going to be here for the business part of this, and I know somebody that I think would be good." And so Betty Mittag came and applied, and I hired Betty, who stayed seventeen years.

By that time, though, when we hired Betty, I needed the space that the divorcement counsellor was using, and we just took the board out that had blocked the window, and you could get to the office through the main part of the house. We had some boxes that had been used in a production of *Man of La Mancha* that are part of the stage boxes that are used in that show, painted a bright yellow, and used them as steps to come in and out of the window into the office.

I had this feeling that my life was over because the main thing I had done for the last twenty-seven years was raise children, keep house, and make things easy so Ben could write, whether we were living in Raleigh, in Charlotte, in Sumter, in Austria—wherever it was. And while I had occasionally done a show, some costumes, or something like that, I had never done anything with a permanent feeling, that this is life. And I felt like, well, what am I really going to do? The shop had started, but it was just beginning. Joel was married. Mike had said he was going to get married. John was in college over at Chapel Hill. So I had an empty nest. And one day I got a phone call from Frances Erdahl, for whom the Erdahl-Cloyd Union at NC State is named.

The Erdahl-Cloyd Union would bring in fine music groups, major orchestras, and the community all over Eastern North Carolina bought tickets, a dollar a concert. You bought a season ticket, which had six or eight concerts. It was all done at Reynolds.

Anyway, the Erdahls went to West Raleigh Presbyterian. And Frances called me one day and said, "Would you consider letting me put your name in the pot to be a deacon?" The first woman deacon had actually been elected while I was in Austria. She had been a friend of my mother's, Cybil Pearce.

And I said, "I really never had thought about it."

And she said, "Well, I would like for you to think about this, and I'll talk to you again." So I thought about this, and I thought, well, that may be what I'm supposed to be doing, this thing that just came out of the blue. She said, "The deacons keep up with the physical needs of the church. The elders take care of the spiritual needs of the church. And I think you'd be good in that position. You've got some time on your hands." So, ultimately, I did say I would.

I was the only woman in the ordination class that year, and my parents were both still alive. They came when I was ordained.

My father had always supported me in anything I wanted to do. He didn't say, "You can't be an engineer because you're a girl." He was more apt to say, "This is the way it works. This is how this road is done." Even as a little kid, he would take me to see roads being built, and I used to say that I wanted to go with him to go see a steam shovel spit dirt.

At the end of the service, he was speaking to the minister and he said, "I'm concerned that my daughter was not properly ordained, because I noticed in all of your comments, you talked to 'those men.'" It certainly brought the minister on his heels, because he has three daughters and he's always very supportive of women doing anything they want to.

So that's how I became a deacon and was put on the budget, finance, and stewardship committee, and the chairman was transferred three months. That must have been maybe '78.

My father, by that time, he had retired from the highway department and gone into business with my mother's brother down in Goldsboro in a liability and insurance company, and he primarily helped contractors get their insurance and what they would need, and all, because of his experience as an engineer.

He talked to me, and he said, "One of the things that I noticed is that churches are never fully insured. I think you should talk to the board of deacons about getting enough insurance for the replacement value." So I became the chairman of that committee and did promote the idea that we should increase our insurance for replacement value, instead of just a percentage. And it was passed. That was the year the church burned, so it was a very good thing we had that insurance.

West Raleigh has always been known as something of an activist church. We had a Sunday school class that discussed current events or things of current interest that often is led by somebody from the University. I remember we had a session on what happens when minimum wage is raised, who benefits and who gets laid off and how long it takes for those people to be benefited again. We had an economist from over at State to come and talk about it. There was also a Trappist monk from the Trappist monastery at Oxford, North Carolina, who several times came and talked to us, and the rabbis from Temple Beth Or have been there.

When the veterans were returning back to school after the second World War, man named Hasses, who was a professor over at NC State, started a series of classes at West Raleigh. I wasn't living here at the time. I was off at school. He noticed a lot of veterans were coming back and going back to college, but their wives were getting a job doing anything they could, and they were going to need some feeding of the mind to keep up with these guys. So he started this Sunday school class for adults that was a discussion. Sometimes it would be a popular book. I know once for that class I did several sessions on Jack Spong, the liberal bishop in the Episcopal Church who had been a paperboy for Ben and me when he was growing up.

At West Raleigh Presbyterian, the synod or the presbytery always supported a minister to be there just for Presbyterian students in the area. Those students don't always come on Sunday mornings—in fact they seldom do—but they are active in the student groups there, and the church supports them. There is a big rec room. Before exams students can go there for quiet to study, and there are usually sort of "nose bag" lunches for them—that's a Girl Scout term. Those are the sort of bags that go over a horse's nose so he could eat without being hitched. So these would be paper bags with maybe fruit and a power bar and a cold drink or something like that in them. And later, on Wednesday nights for three dollars, students could go there and have a substantial meal. Guy Munger's daughter Bridgette used to cook for them, and Bridgette is a wonderful cook. When Bridgette started cooking, the attendance and membership of the students went from being about forty to about seventy-five.

The nice thing is that anybody who has a meeting at the church on the same night could also go there to eat, so lots of times on Wednesday, if I had a meeting there, I would go up there to eat. And it's not only that it's a nice meal, but it's also sort of interesting to eat with the students and sit at the table there and hear what they have to say and what they are talking about. Sometimes they are a little reticent, and then we just sit around for a few minutes. Over a few months, you start to know some of them, and then they lighten up and express some of their concerns and what they are thinking about in the world.

Willard Bennett was an elder at West Raleigh, but I had known him because he had been an officer before, and of course he had been on the Boy Scout troop committee at one time. Ben was the Boy Scout leader there and Willard's two sons were part of the troop, so our boys had known each other.

Anyway, when you become an officer in the Presbyterian church, you go before a committee of elders who ask you a few questions about your religious life and beliefs, and the main thing you have to agree with is the sovereignty of God, but otherwise you have a lot of leeway as long as you can back it up with what you're thinking. Presbyterians do a lot of thinking in committee.

Willard was on this committee for me, and we would occasionally see one another, just as I would see other members of the congregation at the Little Theater or Friends of the College, at plays or at the symphony, things like that. I knew many of the same interests. I also knew he had come to Raleigh as part of the deal when North Carolina State University became the first university in the area to have a new nuclear reactor. And his deal was he would come if he didn't have to teach any undergrad classes. He only wanted to teach graduate students. I think that was 1960 because it was about the same time that Ben and I arrived here from South Carolina.

He didn't tolerate fools very well, and he was a super-intelligent person. One of his colleagues once told me, "You know, Willard Bennett can have a thousand ideas and nine hundred ninety-nine of them you can throw out because they are so off-the-wall, but, ah, that one..." I know that I have read in papers about him that it was said that he "saw beyond the horizon." He did things like predicting the Van Allen belts before they were shown to actually exist; these were these things that go around the world that were found when the astronauts go into space. He invented the radio mass spectrometer before there was any use for it. It was and still is in the nose cone of everything that goes into space to let them know what gasses are in space. He invented the tandem Van de Graaff. This is a way of speeding up electrical particles. They told me out at Los Alamos that without that speed-up of the particles inside of atoms that nothing they did out there would be possible. There's these huge towers out there. And I've also been told that he hasn't gotten credit for things that he should simply because he was hard to deal with.

So he called and said, "I would like to come and pay a purely social call." He wanted to be sure that I understood this wasn't on some church business. And we began to go out together.

I later told him he ought to write a book reassuring older men. When we first started going out, I asked my friend Gert Bliss, Larry's mother, how old she thought Willard was, and she said, "I think he took early retirement. I think he retired at sixty-two." He had only been retired for two years, so I thought he was about sixty-five, just ten years older than me. In fact, he was twenty-five years older. But when you get older, that much age difference doesn't make that much of a difference.

When Willard was a little boy, the story about him is that, for one thing, he was experimenting with chloroform on his sister's cat. The cat died. Still, years later when I first met her, she said, "You better watch him. He killed my cat," which I thought was a nice sibling memory.

Another time, he mixed up something in his room and almost gassed everybody in the family.

How Long Do You Cook Potatoes?

His father had been building an office for himself out in the yard, but Willard came home from school one day and found a sign on it that said, "Bennett's Lab." He was told that, from then on, he was to do all his lab experiments there.

Their house had been a way station on the Underground Railroad, which I thought was sort of interesting as to how the generations change. My great grandparents had all been slave owners. Half of the house was gone. One half of the house had been kept and turned into apartments. The front half had been torn off at some point and a laundromat built there, and people in town were still talking about how awful it was that no one preserved that house with its history. Willard said he could remember as a child being told not to go through these secret passages in the house. The passages were useful because it allowed them to have places where they could run pipes for central heat and indoor plumbing, but originally his room was one of the rooms that whichever runaway slaves would have stayed in. This was in Ohio right at Lake Erie.

His father had owned a company that made batteries and re-wired generators, and he had actually been very much involved with Edison and with the Fords. I've been through Willard's brother's lab at his house, and the thing that was the most fun to see there was that he had collected the old Edison players, the kind that played the spools, and I didn't know that those even had different-sized spools. It's sort of like you had record players that played 78s and then you them that played 45s. When we went to the Edison Museum, Willard was showing me some stuff that they had donated, various lights and generator parts that had been a sort of joint venture at some point, and there was at that time there was still a Bennett Electric Company there with his father's picture on the wall.

Willard's father also had re-married late in life, so his widow was still alive when Willard and I met. I said to him, "When you marry a man who is seventy-eight-years old, you don't expect to have a mother-in-law," but I did.

His grandfather, incidentally, had written some of the hymns and taught at Oberlin music school. Willard had played a violin growing up. Evidently, all of his family had done some sort of music, that he could remember. There would be sort of musicale-type evenings at home, with everybody playing music or singing.

Before coming to Raleigh, Willard had lived in the Washington area because he was involved with naval research; je was a retired military colonel. He had been called up before the Second

How Long Do You Cook Potatoes?

World War because he was the only PhD in the reserves, and he started doing various kinds of research a year before we were actually in the war.

He and his wife at that time split, and then he remarried. So the wife he came to North Carolina with was a different wife. And then they had split. She was never involved in West Raleigh. I didn't know her. I knew their children because he brought the children to church.

Ben and Willard were very different sort of people. Willard was so tied-up with his research in physics that he really didn't have a whole lot of other interests other than music. And he could never be separated from his lab. I told him his kitchen looked like a lab. One time he asked me how long I cooked potatoes, and I said, "Until they're done." I would stick a fork in a potato to see if it was done.

And he said, "Well, I cook mine seven and a half minutes."

And I said, "I never cook anything a half a minute!" But other than that, actually on the Myers-Briggs we scored very much the same. That was the only particular point we differed.

He had gotten very deaf because one of the research things he did during the war. Willard had a lab in Australia and was trying to find ways of getting radio waves out in big electrical storms. So he had an airplane and a crew assigned to him. They would deliberately fly into storms to be struck by lightning and try to send out radio signals, and this was before they knew loud noises hurt your eardrums.

Willard really did not like to go into a crowd. He liked one-on-one or where the group knew that he wasn't hearing real well. He called the Hasses class his "club," and that was really the only group of people I saw him be involved with. If they had something at the university, some sort of reception, he might go and make an appearance, but he never stayed. But he liked to go over to Durham once a month. At Duke, they would bring in a very prominent scientist to speak, and he liked to go there, and I would go with him. Most of the time it was a good thing I had him along coming home so he could tell me what they had talked about, because I had no idea. This was science on a level that was way beyond me. But there again, he had his mind focused on one person, and we always sat right at the front. And I'm sure that he'd gotten to be pretty good at lip reading.

Of the two or three men I went out with after Ben died, Willard was the only one that the dog Lady acknowledged. She growled at every other man that came in the house. And then Willard came in. I remember the dog went and just leaned against him. I figured Willard was serious when he called me one day and said, "Come to supper tonight, and you can bring the dog because I've had the yard fenced."

You know, other people have flowers. Other people are taken on a cruise. Willard took me to Disney World when he found I had never been. He had been there as a chaperone for a bunch of his kids and their friends one time. I don't remember which one of their graduating classes it was, but they said that all of them loved to have him as a chaperone because he was so deaf, he didn't hear all their noise.

I didn't know until I had been dating him for some time that he was twenty-five years older than I was. I didn't know that he had been married before. I knew that he had been in the military, but all the men I knew had been in the military in the Second World War. That was my generation. So that didn't clue me that he was older.

The children of his that I had known were the ones that lived here—Charlie, Ward, and Becky. But Willard took me around to meet all of his other children, who really didn't know each other because his earlier divorces had been not very nice. There were children who were my age. I never counted how many grandchildren there were. But as I met his children out on the West coast, I realized how much alike they all were, that they would really like each other if they knew each other.

He had another interesting sister—not the one whose cat he murdered. She earlier had taught dance during the '20s at the Pasadena Playhouse and rode in some of the early Rose Bowl parades on some of the floats. Later she designed floats for it. She married a man and moved to Oregon where they had a farm, and then Willard's brother started building houses that she designed. Willard also had a brother who came up with something that Willard said, had it been developed, probably would have been better for tracking planes landing than radar was even, but it was the end of the war so there was no reason to develop it further.

When Willard proposed, I told him I still felt married, and I think that is true of a lot of women who are widowed, men too. It takes you a while. I read a lot with my Stephen Ministry stuff about people who have been widowed, either "grass or sod." "Sod" is they died, and "grass" is divorce. I watched my friends being both kinds of widows. I think it is easier to be a "sod widow." You get your life back quicker afterward than grass, because grass means you were rejected.

Coming around to consider Willard's proposal was just a gradual sort of thing. I began to think about, well, I could walk out and be run over by a car tomorrow, and here is a man that I share a lot of interests with. Our children seem to get along okay. Am I throwing away happiness simply because I don't want to be widowed again? And so I said, yes, I would marry him. It was three years after Ben had died. He had been courting me about two years by that point. I went again to Europe that summer, and when I got back I told him I would marry him.

We didn't have any major conflict points that often happen with a second marriage. Neither one of us had any particular money worries. Our children were grown. I told Willard that, if we were married, I would be his last wife, that I wasn't putting up with it any other way. We did sign a prenup agreement, and I made sure that all of my children and all of his children knew this. This was in '81. I wanted my children to know he wasn't after my money and I wasn't after his.

My father died that year. It was the October right after Willard and I had been married in August. In fact, he died the same day that Ben had died, in October. He had cancerous tumors in the tube that goes from your kidneys down to your bladder.

It had first been diagnosed actually while we were in Europe in 1964, but I remember the day that they had operated on him in Chapel Hill and came and told us that they had felt they had gotten everything, that he was going to be okay. Sure enough, he did live another fifteen or so years. It was the same day that Ben got the call saying the Literary Guild had bought *Look Away, Look Away*. That was quite a day of celebration. That was in '63 or '64, something like that.

The cancer re-developed finally, re-metastasized, I guess they call it. And he had a brother who was a doctor, who said the type of thing he had was a very slow-growing cancer, which was one of the reasons it hadn't given him more trouble until right at the end.

My father loved to play golf. That last year of his life, he stopped playing golf. There were computers just coming out then. Joel said he realized how sick paw-paw was when he didn't buy a computer and kept on using his slide rule. He was an engineer, and they used to laugh and say he probably even used a slide rule instead of an alarm clock. He could do anything with a slide rule, figure anything.

How Long Do You Cook Potatoes?

Chapter Thirteen
My Willard Bear

Willard had a house out in Cary, which was a nice little house. It was one of the first that was built out there when they first started developing, just off of Seabrook Avenue. It wasn't big enough for us to have a gathering there, and one of the things we agreed before we married was that we would sell both our houses and buy a house together. But we were kind of side-tracked on that because interest rates went sky high and both of us had paid-for houses, and it's very hard to sell a paid-for house when somebody's going to have to finance it from scratch. It's much better if they are going to buy an older house that they can take care of somebody's loan that has a lower interest rate.

So we were sort of trapped for a while. I rented my house and moved there with him. I left some of my furniture in my old house, and Ruth Bicket and her husband Mark lived there with their two boys. They split, and Mark ended up with the house and he continued there with his second wife. An interesting quirk in North Carolina law is that, when I sold it to them, Willard had to sign the deed, even though he had never lived in the house and never paid on it, just because we were married.

Then, when interest rates came down some, we began to go house hunting. Willard was really very attached to that house. He had sort of designed it. The kitchen particularly was the way he liked it. Of course, I didn't cook in it.

One night after we had looked at places, he said, "I don't like having a basement at all." I do like a basement.

And I said, "Ok, we are going to write down a list of what each one of us can't live without." So I would walk around, carrying this paper with me, and we would evaluate each house against whatever the paper said.

Anyway, we saw this house on St. Mary's Street, and he really liked it. I thought he was going to move in with the people right then. I finally said, "These people want to eat supper. We've got to go."

We talked about it that night, and he said, "You know, I think it's over-priced. Let them worry a little bit, and we'll see if they come down."

Well, they were building a house, and it got to the point that they had to show the builder that they had sold their current house. So a friend of mine who was a realtor called me and said, "They've come down to Willard's price because they've got to have something on this house."

In the meantime, Willard had gotten sick with shingles. I told him they'd come down, and he said, "Ugh, I have to think about this..." I knew he felt awful, so I just went down and I put money on it because I knew he liked the house.

The time came to move, and I said the movers were coming. I'd been packing stuff, and I said, "Do you want me to help you with stuff in your office?"

And he said, "I thought you bought that house for an investment."

And I said, "No, the mover is coming Monday morning. If you are living with me and still married to me, I expect you to be ready to move."

I had learned a certain amount from dealing with Ben. He had a sort of Germanic attitude, sort of in a daze most of the time, and somebody had to keep things going. So he might come in the middle of how things are going and make suggestions. Ben said he would have lived in a cave had he not married. He made that admission.

In some ways, Willard had the same sort of being off in left field much of the time. That the creative mind, whether it's an artistic creative mind or a scientific creative mind, in many ways it works the same. So I think that is one reason I got along better with Willard than his other wives. There was also the fact that I didn't have the resentment toward his spending so much time in the lab and not being available to help with children and things. I could see that that would have been an annoyance.

The other thing was that not only did he keep track of whether or not he'd cooked potatoes seven-and-a-half minutes, he kept a whole box of little tiny notebooks that recorded every penny he spent. I said that only time I do that is when I'm changing currency. For a little while, to make the currency become real money, I'll write down how much I'm spending.

And I said, "I'm not spending your money on things that I know we'll split. I will write that down. I'll keep a list of that."

Once a month we got together and sat down with what we had spent money on that was for both of us—who paid the gas bill or who paid the water bill, sometimes one of us and sometimes the other—and just added them up. And sometimes I owed him ten dollars, and sometimes he owed me ten dollars, and we never had any words over it, but when we first got married, he said, "I'll give you a clothing allowance."

My Willard Bear

And I said, "I don't want any man to ever tell me how much I can spend on clothes."

And he said, "I guess that means that you can't tell me what to spend on clothes," because I had chided him once. He was wearing such a ratty-looking jacket to some place that I didn't think he should be wearing such a ratty-looking jacket.

And I said, "Well, I guess it does." So we never argued over clothing again.

Like most scientists and writers—creative people—he didn't think much about clothes, although he did like plaid. And he liked to wear a bow tie, and he liked an old sweater. I have a teddy bear that I saw once in a store window after he had died that I had to go in and buy because this teddy bear was wearing glasses and a plaid bow tie and a sort of Mr. Rogers sweater with leather elbows. And all he needed was the red beret; Willard always wore a red beret. So I made the bear a red beret. That's my Willard bear.

When Willard and I first got married, I was still involved with a lawsuit with a publishing company that had illegally published some of Ben's books, a copyright suit. It was to be heard in Wake County court, and Willard, I didn't ask him to come with me. It seemed to me that he would feel out of place doing that. So I didn't expect him, but at the end, when I came out victorious with this suit, I looked around, and there in the courtroom was Willard, sitting in the back. It was a pouring-down rainy day, so he had his plaid London Fog and not the red beret this day but a plaid billed cap. And a plaid shirt. And a plaid jacket. And a plaid bowtie. And I'm afraid that I made a rather tactless statement because I said, "Well what about plaid pants?"

And he said, "I think plaid pants are loud." So I realized he never wore plaid pants.

Willard's daughter Becky always kids Joel and Mike and John and says they owe her because she's given me two grandchildren. Logan was born after Willard and I were married. Willard and I used to keep Logan if Becky and her husband Scott went off somewhere, so one of my favorite pictures is Willard, sitting in a chair in the living room there by the fire, and Logan is sprawled on the floor in front of the fire with crayons and papers all around him. Logan must have been about four, maybe five.

Then Corey was born after Willard died, and I used to keep Corey some too. Corey was not as easy-going a child as Logan. Logan, just whatever came up, whatever you've got on the table to eat, he wants to try it, and I can remember him sitting in the kitchen doing experiments. Becky would let him have a big bowl, and he would pour all sorts of things from the kitchen into this bowl and stir them up and see what would happen. So I was not surprised when he majored in chemistry at NC State.

Becky's mother was still alive when Logan was born, and one of the things that I wanted to be sure of was that nobody thought I was trying to take her place. And so Becky had asked me what Logan should call me. This was right after he was born. I had given this some thought earlier, about people who have "Grandmother Something" with the last name and "Grandmother Something" with another last name, and I thought, no, no, I don't want to be that. I want to be Oma, which is the German term or at least it's what Austrian's use. Germans also say *grossmutter*, but little Austrian children say *oma* and *opa* for grandmother and grandfather.

So I said, I would be Oma. Oddly enough, when Becky's youngest son Corey came along, he couldn't quite make that sound, so for quite a while I was "Ooma." And the children of Willard's son Ward call me that too. The other kids in the family were all much older, so the Michael twins say "Doug." They were about ten-years old the first time I met them.

Anyway, with Logan, it was exciting to have this little baby, and as he grew, oddly enough, he was very much like Joel had been as a child. He had the same boundless energy, just an interest in everything. All children have some of that, but there was a little different edge to it, like this thing of just trying out what's going to happen if you just mix up all this stuff in the kitchen. As he got older, I would sometimes say, "Joel, he's so much like you." Joel would get very exasperated.

Logan also picked up a very large vocabulary, which my boys also had. I remember there was a reception down at Joel's when he had a studio downtown, and a friend of mine was looking at the columns, which were strangely built, which held up the roof there. And she turned to Logan and she said, "They are interesting columns, aren't they, Logan?"

And Logan was about eight at the time, seven or eight, and he said, "Yes, they are, but my favorite are Corinthians."

I took him one time to Peace College, and Sally Buckley, the writer, was there. And I introduced us. I said, "This is my grandson." We were going to see Midsummer Night's Dream. So Sally Buckley said to him, "Well, I hope you enjoy this."

And he said, "Yes, I rather prefer it over Romeo and Juliet." He had his hands behind his back sort of like I'd seen his grandfather do. "I rather prefer it..." I could see Joel having made these same sorts of statements at that age.

Willard did like little children. He was chairman of the board of deacons at West Raleigh, and he said that he always felt like one of the statements a church makes is how it cares for its children. He was very much in favor of West Raleigh having a daycare center, of any church having a daycare center. I'm sure it would have upset him terribly when he realized we no longer were able to have the daycare center because, frankly, it had been too big a success and we did not have the space that would be required for that size daycare center and for the programs we had, nor would a smaller group of children been able to financially support this center. So we had to close it, but at the same time we still have the yard there with play areas for the kids so that, if they are not going to church or during vacation Bible school when older kids are there too, there is some space for them for play. But we had gotten to the point that the children were having to take their naps upstairs, and it's no longer allowed for kids to be on a second floor because they need to have a way to simply walk out of the building in case of fire. We were very much aware of the danger of fire and how that can come on when you least expect it because of the fire we'd had there.

So we reluctantly closed the center. The space is just used as Sunday school classrooms now. But we are part of a group of twelve churches giving space for families who are homeless. During the day, they can go to a place where there are computers and phones and people to help them look for jobs and homes. The churches set up one of the Sunday school classrooms for each family as a bedroom and provide supper and breakfast the next morning and have food there so they can pack a lunch. Every week, a different church does this, every three months. You just have it for a week, and the beds and blankets and sheets and all that sort of thing that are moved from one church to another.

Some of the families have two parents and sometimes there is only one. Sometimes there are babies and they need a crib. Sometimes there will be lots of children. I've gone sometimes in the evening if they think they are going to have a lot of small children. I'll go and read stories to them in the evening. The kids are given a space to do their homework, and they can use the library there if they want to have something to read for a book report because there still is a large children's library there for the children of the church.

We do this through Urban Ministries. When they finally get a job, they go through another program that's called Step-Up that helps them. For three or four months, they are given a furnished apartment, which they pay for, but the money is saved. The churches actually pick up all the tab for the utilities and whatnot, and, at the end of the three or four months, that money is returned to them to use for deposits so they can get their own apartment and get their own utilities turned on because often that's the biggest problem.

The other program that operates there that also uses some of this is something called Wheels for Hope. People donate a car, and there are a bunch of people there who like to work on cars. They get them running and shine them up. If a family needs a car then, they can be recommended and the car with be sold to them—it's financed to them—and for a year they have the use of the garage there and people to help them keep it running too.

There is a little service, a little ceremony, when they come to pick up the car. I've been there a couple of times for this, and it's nice. The car is blessed, and they are given a bucket with all the things in it to help keep the car clean and for an oil change. And the church tries to order a book on maintenance for that particular car, that sort of thing. They get cars sometimes that really wouldn't be appropriate for this. Sometimes you are donated a Rolls Royce or you are donated a car that is going to cost too much for them to keep it in running shape. With something that runs ten miles to the gallon or something like that, you're not doing the family any service. So two or three times a year they have a big car auction and the money raised from that helps support the program.

Anyway, I like learning new things. I'm turned on by brains. And I was learning new things with Willard. I've been to the mass acceleration labs at Boeing and had Willard there to explain what it's all about. And I've been to the power plant that's on the fault out there at Diablo Canyon. I went with him for one of the standard tours, and it was wonderful to see how relieved this little tour guide felt when we left, because Willard had questions to ask her that she had no idea how to answer and so would try to rush us along.

But he loved to travel like that. He had a good attitude toward travel too, that if you find something interesting, stay there and look at it. I know we were driving up the West Coast and there is a place out there in California where the majority of the seeds used in the United States are developed and sown. There are just fields and fields of flowers blooming that are just raised for their seed. And we ended up staying there a couple of days. We thought we were just going to have lunch there, but it was just so breath-taking to see these acres and acres of different flowers. There would be a place half the size of Meredith college that was all yellow flowers, and right beside that a place that size all with blue flowers, and then another place right next to it with just these little roads between them.

He was interested in American Indians. I've camped at Mesa Verde National Park. I've visited The Four Corners. Willard liked to take pictures, and we were at The Four Corners—you know, this is where the four states come together—and at that time it wasn't a major tourist attraction as it seems to have become now, but there were a few Indians there with tables out, selling little "made in Japan" Indian novelties. The main thing that was there—plus the fact that there is this big round piece in the ground that is marked as to which state is where—were four porta potties, one in each state, and Willard thought this was so funny that he got out his camera, and he wanted to be sure to get a good picture, so he got out his tripod and set the whole thing up. By the time we had left, everybody there had realized this was funny, and everybody there was taking pictures of The Four Corners porta-potties.

Anyway, Willard's brother Paul and his brother's wife Katie were going to celebrate their fiftieth wedding anniversary. So we were flying to the west coast to see them in California, but we decided to fly to Denver and pick up a car there and drive the rest of the way and visit some national parks; Willard was good at arranging a trip.

The year before, we had been in New Mexico. I told Ward that we had been on the mile-high highway, and Willard had just sort of dozed constantly on that. And his son Ward said, "I think the altitude was too high for him. He wasn't getting enough oxygen."

So before we went on this trip, I said, "Ward, he wasn't to go to all these high-rise parks."

And Ward said, "Well, try to talk him into coming down lower if he begins to not feel well." So we had driven to Zion, which was really un-like any other range of mountains I had ever seen. I really like Zion Park. All these parks have cabins you can rent that are usually nicely set up so that you can fix a cup of coffee or keep a bottle of booze there. There's usually sort of a kitchenette, and then there is a restaurant right there in the park. But usually the little cabins are very private.

The year before, at Mesa Verde, we had stayed at one of these, and the deer there, I guess they get accustomed to people. We were sitting on the deck to this little cabin and eating peaches and would throw the peels down. The mother deer came, and she had twin fawns. She came closer and closer. I held my hand out and she ate pieces of peach right from my hand. It was kind of a thrill having a wild animal do that.

Anyway, we flew into Denver and started driving, and we got into Zion and he didn't feel well. We were there on Sunday. And he said, "Well, you go and explore. I just don't think I'm going to go out today." And I knew that wasn't good.

I went and found a payphone and called Ward. And he said, "It sounds like altitude sickness has got him. Try to get him down to a lower altitude."

And I said, "Well, we had planned to drive down to the Grand Canyon tomorrow."

And he said, "That's not much lower, but it's a little bit lower. Keep an eye on him and give me a call tomorrow." Willard had told Ward that we would call a couple of times along to road to tell him we were okay, and Ward tried to convince him then to get down a little lower. He didn't pay much attention to Ward. After all, Ward was his little boy.

So we started driving to the Grand Canyon. Willard usually drove in the morning and I'd drive in the afternoon. That day, I said, "Well, you aren't feeling very good. I'll drive this morning." I realized that he was doing the same thing as before, just sort of blanking out.

When we got close to the Grand Canyon, I just pulled into a little town. He didn't even wake up. I pulled into a motel and got us a room and asked how to get hold of a doctor or where there was an emergency room. And he said, "You need to go about forty miles on to the Grand Canyon."

I thought, well, I'm not going to do that, so I called Ward and Ward said, "I think the best thing to do is to come home. I'll make the arrangements from here."

The next morning, we drove down to Phoenix to catch a plane to take us to where we could then catch a real plane down into Raleigh, but I remember the airline people, how nice they were. And the rental car people said, "Just leave the car there. We'll get the car."

I remember the only plane out of there was one of these little "puddle jumpers," and Willard said, "I'm not flying on that. It's dangerous."

And I said, "Look, it has two engines, and you flew all over the South Pacific in a plane with one engine and Japanese shooting at you. This doesn't look anything like that dangerous. Come on. I'm not driving any further." So he got on the plane, and Ward met us and had arranged for Willard's doctor to see us in the morning, and he put him in the hospital.

He was doing really well, and I remember he was standing up, shaving, and he said, "I think they're going to let me go this afternoon or tomorrow." The next morning, when I went out there, he had had a stroke, and he died the next day.

Willard died in September of '87. It was right at the end of September. The funeral was in October. Ben was actually buried on Halloween Day. My father had died in October. So October has not been a real good month for me, between Halloween and family funerals.

We were married about eight years, and the interesting thing is that in some ways I had the reactions that widows have more after Willard's death than I did after Ben's, because when Ben and I would go out, we would go to a party and we didn't stick together. We would each work a different part of the room, sort of like politicians, I guess. Then Ben would go off on a research trip somewhere, and we never travelled together to Europe except when we went by ship. We never went on the same plane. The only time we ever flew anywhere together was when he was giving some talks to the Ohio Electric Co-op people after he wrote *The Last Valley*. Since we had a couple of good friends who had moved out to Ohio, Mike and John and he and I flew up and stayed with them while he went on over to the convention they were having. There still was a little bit of feeling of that plane could go down. You have to remember, this was the '60s and '70s, but I think it was more that each of us had different things that we saw to.

Willard's hearing was very bad, and he liked to have me close by to make sure he understood what the conversation was about. So it was harder for me to go places alone after Willard died than it had been after Ben died, even though Ben and I had been married twenty-seven years. I had the feeling that Ben was just somewhere else.

There's also the Neil Simon play *Second Time Around* where the man's wife has died and they had been living in Paris. He was back in Paris and he saw an antique shop, and he said because this was one of the ones she would have gone in, that he went in almost as if he expected to find her there. And I remember having a similar experience in Brussels. I was taking the boat train to England and had a day in Brussels, and I saw a gun shop in Brussels that was selling antique guns. I went in and realized I had the same feeling, because I was sort of checking it out for Ben.

My Willard Bear

It was too bad that Willard never knew that he was even being considered to be installed into the Inventors Hall of Fame, which is in Akron, OH. It's part of the Smithsonian. They contacted me and he was inducted into that hall of fame in '91, so that would have been about three years after he had died. I went up and made the acceptance speech for the family and was royally treated by the people there. Becky and Scott went and they too were royally treated. They took Logan with them. And there was to be a very formal reception. Ward went. Harry did not come. I think Harry was still in school. But I had gotten tuxedos, or I think tails for Scott, but Ward was wearing a tux, and Logan said, "What shall I wear?"

And his mother said, "We'll get you a nice sport coat."

And Logan said, "But they're wearing formal clothes." He was about eight or nine. So I got him a set of tails which we later used in the shop as Abraham Lincoln for a little boy. But he had a brand-new pair of snakeskin cowboy boots which he wore with it because it was the first pair of snakeskin cowboy boots he had ever owned.

Willard was inducted for his invention of the radio mass spectrometer, which is still used in the nose cone of everything that goes into space. In fact, John Glenn presented it. I have the medal on a ribbon and all. In Glenn's speech, he said, "This goes to a man's invention that went into space before I did."

Chapter Fourteen
You Broads

Raleigh Creative Costumes moved to St. Mary's Street, where it stayed many years before we moved to Hillsborough Street across from Meredith College right up until our last day.

Jimmy Thiem I had known for years. He was older than I. In the late '30s and early '40s he was running a record department at his dad's office supply store. To buy a record, you went down and you could listen to them, but by the time my age group got around to buy a record, we were buying it because we had already heard it somewhere. Jimmy was big on promoting things on radio. In fact, he is credited with being the person who promoted Andy Griffith's *What It Was, Was Football*, getting it played on radio stations all over the country. Radio was big then. He would go to New York and see the shows, see what was going to be the big thing, to give him an idea of what records to buy.

He also promoted Ava Gardner. He said he took her to the first major dance she'd ever been to and told her what to wear and how to behave and whatnot. He was probably in his mid-twenties by then, maybe a little older. I don't think he took her out as any kind of date. It wasn't a romantic thing. It was just that he saw her as a girl who could use some polish, and all of his life he had a certain amount of that. Down at the shop at times, we'd get a little sloppy, and he'd say, "All right, gals. Stand up straight! Where's your lipstick today?" Of course nowadays he would be considered as having trouble working with women because he always referred to us as "you broads." Not only was it a different era, but it was Jimmy.

Jimmy did not move his store down to the Cameron Village Shopping Center when Cameron Village opened up. He stayed downtown, and downtown died. He closed the record shop, and that, I think, just about killed him. I did not know him during that time, but his wife Rebecca told me that. He went to work at Raleigh Office supply, which was down the street from the costume shop's St. Mary's Street location.

Well, one day I was saying something about how it was in September that I was looking for people to come to work, and Rebecca said, "Well, I bet Jimmy would love to do it." I said I just paid minimum wage for people who come in and do that. She said, "I think he'd have fun doing that. I think he'd do it." So he started coming in. We stayed open until 9 PM for Halloween, and he'd come over after Raleigh Office Supply had closed. Then he started coming in on Saturdays. Then anytime there was a holiday or he otherwise wasn't working at Raleigh Office Supply, he would walk in, and I left him to do most of the office work that went on then.

He was wonderful. There were so many times when I would have a teacher come in who was not a theater person but had simply been told that, because she taught vocal music or English, she should put on a play or a musical. She would come in for advice, and Jimmy would pull up—out of all this background he had—shows that he had seen and directors that he had worked with. The first thing he would say is, "What voices do your guys have?" if she was doing a musical, and then he would pull up some show that nobody had thought about doing in years that would fit the voices and the sort of crew she had and her abilities.

He really didn't get credit for the theater stuff he did. Part of it was because on stage he would drive you crazy. He really didn't take directions very well. I guess he wanted to be in charge. He knew he wasn't a director, but you never were real sure exactly where Jimmy was going to be standing or which way he was going to turn or really if he had all his lines down. But he was very big in the theater. He also was very much involved with the guy who directed *Dreamgirls* on Broadway. He would invite Jimmy and Rebecca to come up, and they would stay several days and see whatever his new show was.

Jimmy and Rebecca were good friends with Ainsley Pryor, who was here as a director in the '50s and then went out to Hollywood and died very young. Ainsley's wife and Rebecca were close friends, and, oddly enough, I had just opened a custom clothing shop when they were here and his wife was pregnant. I designed and made a bunch of maternity clothes for her. In fact, Rebecca was laughing about those maternity clothes one of the last times I saw her, how they made the rounds, which was what maternity clothes used to do. Rebecca said she remembered wearing them too. Dad used to say that maternity and baby clothes were Communism in America.

Jimmy was the most wonderful Santa. He did Santa at the Carolina Country Club for years—very "old Raleigh," which Jimmy was. He was a member of the Terpsichorean Club.

As Santa Claus, he would do private gigs, but one year, he did Santa at Cameron Village—for several years, really—but the one year I went, one of the newspapers sent a reporter out with her child to visit all the Santas at every shopping mall. When it was all over, when they had seen all the Santas in town, the reporter said to her little girl, "Do you know which one was the real one?"

And her kid said, "Yeah. The Santa Claus down there in Cameron Village. That's the real one."

That was Jimmy. And he was the one Santa who didn't give anything. All the other ones gave out lollipops or balloons. He didn't even have a natural beard, but, boy, he worked at that beard to make sure it looked good. And if you were going to have him appear at a party, you had to have a place for him to dress there. He didn't want anyone to see Santa Claus driving up. It was definitely a staged production.

After he passed away, we had the "Jimmy Thiem Memorial Drawer" in the office at Raleigh Creative Costumes for the "Jimmy Thiem Memorial Friday Afternoon Drinking Society." Jimmy had troubles with alcohol. He was in and out of AA later in his life. So if Jimmy couldn't drink with us, we would drink to him on Friday afternoon after the store closed, and sometimes Rebecca, who was working at the dentist's office just up the street on St. Mary's Street, would come down and join us.

Her Words

Suzie worked for me at the shop, and she came from Women's Prison, the first of many women from there who worked for me. She had been Joan Munger's secretary when Joan got a job working at the prison.

Before she was locked up, Suzie made fancy cakes for people at home, and so when she got eligible to be on work release, they talked about her cooking at the Governor's Mansion, but the Governor's people said "no" because Suzie poisoned her husband. So they got her a job at the Velvet Cloak, which was where all the legislators stayed. As Joan said, "She could just knock off the legislature."

Joan said, "You know, Doug, Suzie doesn't really like working down there. You should have her working here at the shop." Well, earlier I had been looking for a bookkeeper, and she said, "I can get you any kind of bookkeeper you want."

And I said, "Joan, this place is the land of fantasy and the last thing these girls need is fantasy. They need reality. I'm not sure this is a good job for them." As I saw it, they just had no idea of the results of whatever they would do. There was no cause-and-effect with them, and for many of them, they'd been in so long. I remember Suzie talking. She said, "I didn't know milk came in different kinds and had a different color top, so you would know if it was one percent or skim milk or whole milk."

But I said, "Well, I'll give her a try." So I did and found out that she was great. She always was on time because they dropped her off. It did worry me that if she got sick during the day, she would have to go back to prison on the bus, and so I got certified to be able to take her in the car, or any other prisoners who were working there later.

Suzie was from up near Greensboro, very pretty—blonde, blue eyes, short, curly hair—and very intelligent. She became a good friend too, so when Frank Lyman, Wat's son, was getting married, Wat invited Suzie to the wedding and the dance reception that would be held afterwards. So Suzie was dancing with one of the groomsmen who said to her, "Where have you been all my life?" That great old line.

Suzie said, because she was perfectly frank about it, "Women's Prison."

And he said, "Oh, yeah. I bet you killed your husband."

And she said, "As a matter of fact, I did." Well, if you want to see a dead stop on the dance floor, you couldn't do much better than that.

One time, police came to the door at the shop and knocked on the door. It had been after closing, and I was just closing the books up and counting the money, that sort of thing, so the door was locked. I went to the door and said, "We're closed," and he held up his badge.

He came in and showed me a picture that he said he'd gotten off a security camera and said, "Is this beard real, or do you think he bought it here?"

I said, "We sell a beard that looks just like that, and I know we only had one gray one left. Let me just look and see if we still have it because I think I saw Suzie selling it to somebody." So I went and looked, and of course it was gone. And I said, "Yes, Suzie sold it."

He said, "I wonder if she'd talk to me then about anything she might know about him."

And I said, "Well, she just lives around the corner and she's probably out walking her dog. I'll give her a call and tell her to stop by."

And he said, "That would be good."

So Suzie stopped by with her dog. At the time, she was on parole, living at Joan's. She had a room there. So she came in and she said, "Oh, yeah, I sold him that. And that's not his hair. I sold him a wig too."

He said, "Do you remember how tall he was?"

She said, "Let's see. This is how high I had to reach to put the wig on him. I'll draw you a picture of him too." She was an excellent artist, and so she did.

And he said, "We have just installed a program down at the station that people can describe a suspect and it will make a picture." This was early on in being able to do that. "I don't know how to run it," he said, "but someone comes in at nine o'clock tonight who knows how. If I send a car around to get you, could I ask you to come down and do that?"

And she said, "Why certainly. My parole officer would be most upset if I didn't." Well, his jaw literally dropped.

When I was packing up to move the shop over to Hillsborough Street, there was a group that was training to go out and apply for jobs and learn what was required for that. So they came and packed up for me, as a group. I couldn't pay them directly. They always had a guard with them, and the guard took their money and then gave each of them a percentage of it. The rest was put in the prison bank to be given them when they were released.

I was on a committee that was from both black and white churches in Raleigh, and we would meet twice a month at the prison to talk about things we might be able to do to make life a little easier for some of them. At that time there was only one eastern North Carolina Women's Prison and one western, so sometimes they would have children that had no way to visit with them, and we would see if we could drum up some transportation.

There used to be a big Christmas tree farm in Warrenton that I loved to go to because it was fun to go out and pick out the tree, and they'd come and cut it down, and you could ride back on the tractor with it. Then they would put the tree on a shaking machine to shake all the trash out of it; birds would have built their nests in there and whatnot, and other trees would lose their leaves in the winter, so there would be those in there too. Then they would net it and put it on top of your car for you. And it didn't matter what size tree you got, it was $20, which was a bargain.

I used to get them for Women's Prison every year. They've got the chapel out there, so I'd get a big tree to go in there until they got a new warden who decided the girls spent too much time decorating it and that they didn't need that big a tree.

I tried to get other business owners to also hire women from prison. I said, "These are the most faithful workers you'll ever hire. They need that job and they need a 'first' job." But I never had any luck getting anybody else to hire any of women from prison.

Chapter Fifteen
Aw, Cuddin'!

At the end of our interviews, I asked Doug some general questions about life, about racial relations and child-rearing and what she thought of all the changes that have happened in North Carolina during her life. Have we been losing our culture or getting over our past?

There is a lot that we are getting over, and it'll take another generation to really get over it. They talk about how long it's taken other warring countries with civil wars to get over it—the British and the Irish—and I think it will take definitely my generation to die off, because we still heard Civil War stories from the survivors.

A lot of the Southern-ness about Raleigh changed when IBM started bringing non-Southerners into North Carolina in 1960 with the Research Triangle. They were known for moving people. IBM was known as "I'm Bein' Moved." But what really made IBM become large here was that, when they would then move people away from North Carolina, they found that so many people actually left IBM to get a job with one of the other Research Triangle companies that were moving in because they didn't want to leave. So IBM just enlarged and made this one of their really big places.

Now, the Southern-ness about other parts didn't. Warrenton is, in some ways, much the same way it was when I was growing up there. I lived in a small town, and I miss that feeling of a small town. I think that in some ways my church began to take that place. It became sort of like a small-town family almost.

In Warrenton, there was a church bell up in the tree of the Presbyterian Church. It would ring and give you about ten minutes, fifteen minutes— I've forgotten how long, exactly—so that you would start walking to church, and then when church would start, the second bell rang.

Lots of things were done that way when it wasn't common for everyone to have a watch. I can remember at Miss Mill's that there were lots of people who ate there. It was a large family. She had seven sons, my father being one of them. There would almost always be one or two visiting that would bring their families. And so some child would go through the house about ten minutes before and ring the bell so that people knew it was time to go to the bathroom and wash their hands before eating, because you could not get up from the table to go do that after the meal had started. Then at the second bell, you came to the table, and you stood and waited until Miss Mill sat down.

If your family sat down together for meals, that's where you learned to behave at a meal, what kind of conversation is acceptable, what kind of behavior is acceptable. As teenagers, as we went into adulthood, I don't think any of us wondered how to behave when we were in more adult situations. I saw an awful lot of teenagers—well, really the age of my kids—being uncomfortable and really not knowing how to behave in adult situations because it hadn't been something that was just ordinarily done. I think people started using the TV and didn't eat all together, so that you didn't really learn to cut your meat properly or to put your napkin in your lap.

With my own children, we always ate together in the evenings, and when Ben used to come home from lunch when we lived in South Carolina, there would be a meal in the middle of the day. We wouldn't always eat breakfast together. In fact, I usually tried not to get Ben up when I was trying to get the children off to school. I'd rather feed them and get them out. He often wrote late into the night.

I think parents should teach their children table manners, before they are five or six. This will stand them well for the rest of their lives, and the only way to do it is to eat with them, together at a table, at least every other day. They get accustomed to it, without having to be told, where the utensils go or how to cut their meat. They learn by observing, and particularly if you have several children, they quickly learn that they don't want to look into their brother or sister's mouth either.

It also gives you an opportunity to talk with the children on a more adult level and find out what they are thinking about. People complain that children come home from school, and you say, "What did you do today?" And the children always say the same old thing. If you're sitting at supper, you can make some comment about the food. "These grow in such-and-such a place." "Where is that?" "Well, let's look at the map..."

A lot of adults, if you ask how their day is, they might not say much. You need to give people a leading question, and children are the same way. It's also good to tell children, before they meet somebody new, what to say, what they are to call these people. "This is your uncle Ron. This doesn't mean he's necessarily your father or mother's brother or sister, but this is an acceptable way for you to speak to that adult." Or, "When you meet Uncle Ron, ask him about being a clown." Give them something, a conversation lead.

My mother did that for me. I remember one thing especially. After we moved to Raleigh, occasionally I would be in Warrenton visiting by myself some parent or friend who had invited me, and I would say, "Mother, what do I call these people? Everybody there knows who I am." I was ten when we moved here, so this would be between the time I was ten and thirteen, because then the war started and there wasn't much visiting back and forth.

And she said, "Well you are probably kin to practically everybody in town. So if they speak to you and you realize that you don't know their name, have a handkerchief or something you can drop. At that point, just before you drop it, say, 'Aw, cuddin'…' And as you get down to pick it back up off the floor, mutter something, and they will think that you've said their name." It works!

I think children have to be trained how to speak with adults. I found that the children who came to the shop to work sometimes had to speak to an adult on an adult sort of level, but they would wait until they are spoken to instead of greeting them when they come in.

Decent table manners can do more for you all through your life than almost any other training, and I used to tell my kids, "I don't care whether you eat with the European manners or the American manners," but it was one or the other.

I had one friend who had that view of letting the child be free to find its own way, and I'll never forget the look on my mother's face when this little girl came up to my mother and looked at her and gave her a "raspberry," instead of just saying, "Hello." But her mother had never told her that's what you do. She was finding her way.

I think children feel more secure when they have some parameters within which to work. I don't mean that you do this all the time, or for every little thing, but I think children need some parameters. We wouldn't have been made parents otherwise. Even dogs and cats teach their children some parameters.

But try not to criticize them. This is something that I see in some children, with parents criticizing them in front of their peers. I remember one little boy who was a good friend of John, who came to spend the summer with us in Austria.

There were two things that I had that were requirements for kids to come. They were to bring a suit, because we would take them out to places where boys would be expected to wear a suit, the opera or the theater, and people dress a little more there, even in the '70s. And the other thing was that I would pay for one telephone call when they had arrived to let their parents know that they had arrived safely. His parents were puzzled as to why he called when he got there. The entire time he was there, nearly two months, he heard from his mother one time. There was nothing from his father or his sister, and in that one letter, she took up the entire letter with the conference she had with German teacher Herr Watts because he had been given an A- instead of an A, and why had he not gotten an A in German? She was lambasting him for her having to go and talk to Philip Watts about this.

Don't do that to your children.

When it came to disciplining a child, I didn't ever object to using my hand on their fanny. They never got bruised or anything, but a hand in an appropriate place. Joel was laughing the other day because of a word he said that he never hear me say but that he hears mothers say to their children now. I can't remember what it is, not "time out." We had, "Go sit in a chair." My mother told me this, "Go sit in a chair." In fact one of the things I saw that she had written in the baby book she kept for me was that I had done something— which she did not record, so I do not know what I had done—but I said, "I'm already sitting in a chair." For my children, if they didn't obey me after the second time they were spoken to, the either got a hand on their fanny or a switch on their legs. This was not negotiated.

My sons are grown now, and not prone to violence. And they all were taught to use a gun when they were five or six years old. We had a pump pistol that my uncle John had taught his son with, and he gave it to Ben to teach Joel. They never had BB guns. By the time they got a gun, it was a .22, and it only was used when they went hunting or target shooting with their father.

I would save all glass bottles, and when children would get to be really obnoxious for seven days in a row, Ben would come and get a bag of glass bottles. There was a big sawdust pile out in the woods somewhere—which has since become a housing development, I'm sure—and he would take them out there and line the bottles up and let them shoot bottles. There's something very satisfying about the sound that you hear when you break that bottle. It channeled their aggression, and they would come back in the best mood.

It's almost like the economic pendulum that swings back and forth, about violence and children. I remember when my children were small, the church they decided that children did not need to be taught the catechism with their stated answers but would let them find these things out. There was an idea that children saying, "Now I lay me down to sleep. I pray the Lord my soul to keep. If I die before I wake, I pray the Lord my soul to take," was frightening to children, but I always noticed those were the children who were less afraid of the dark, because they knew there was a higher power looking after them.

Also all of the Bible stories were sanitized. I was teaching Sunday school for three-year olds in South Carolina, and the material I was given did not even have Bible stories as their base. They just came in and told sort of moral tales, and I thought this was a waste of time, so I ordered some material from somewhere else that had Bible stories in it. But the Bible story books were so sanitized. You know they didn't have Shadrach, Meshach, and Abednego going into the fiery furnace.

And I think in a way some of that has happened again with their stories, and yet they get their violence otherwise in video games or TV. We talk about the violence in German fairy tales. It's nothing compared to the violence that these kids get in TV or whether it's a video game or TV. I don't know if you're familiar with a German fairytale called *Struwwelpeter*. It's a set of moral stories, and the two little boys, Max and Moritz, are very bad. It's all told in rhyme and has kind of traditional illustrations with it. The boys laugh at the tailor in the town and scream, "Schneider! Schneider! Meck-meck-meck!" And they show them then taking a saw and cutting the bridge in two so that Schneider falls in the water. I mean, they do the sort of things that cartoons do. But at the end—this is the part that would never go over now in an American translation—they get tied up in a sack of wheat that's to go to the mill, and the miller mills the sack of wheat. It comes out in the outline of the little boys there, and the ducks come and eat them up. So they get their comeuppance.

When I was a little girl, I grew up in a house that had no central heat, and I wasn't quite three-years old, because we were living over in Durham, when I stepped behind the fire screen to throw something in the fire. It so frightened my mother that she grabbed me and told me the story about the little girl who had done that and ended up there was nothing left but her little red shoes.

In Warrenton there is the old cemetery a little monument that always fascinated me as a child because a little boy had been drowned in a creek near there, and all they found were his hat and shoes. And so there was this monument that looks like a rock, like a sort of rock you could sit on by a creek, and his shoes and hat are on that rock, little high-top buttoned shoes and a straw hat for a little boy, all carved out of stone. That was a reminder to be careful around water. There is an end. Everything doesn't have a happy ending.

Having pets can give you a wonderful opportunity to talk about death. We had a little cemetery in the backyard, and we dug and put some flowers there and talked about the animal. This was death, and I remember saying to the boys when something was deadly dangerous, that if you died or somebody else died, I would cry and cry for days and days.

Sex education—well, some of it you get again if you have pets who haven't been fixed. This brings it up. I'm very much in favor of sex education in school. If you don't have it, people don't know how to avoid needing an abortion, and there were people who had to go to the backdoor abortionist simply because they didn't know any better. I don't think there probably was as much sex in dating when I was a teenager, not because of morals but because birth control was less dependable.

It frightens me when I read about people who are trying to prevent any abortion. I knew two women who had to carry dead fetuses, simply because they would be considered abortions, until they had been pregnant for seven months and doctors could induce labor or Cesarean. That's something I never see discussed, and there was very much an emotional impact. I think the fetus died at about four months, and at somewhere between five or six months she had a spontaneous delivery.

I can't say that we did a great job of sex education. I don't really remember ever sitting down to have "the talk," but I don't remember ever avoiding questions. And we never restricted anything they could read, so certainly by the time they were in fifth grade they were reading adult novels, which was kind of the way Ben and I had both been brought up. We had never been kept to the children's section of the library.

I remember one funny thing that happened one day at the dining room table. My mother was visiting, and I can't remember what came up about some man who had various affairs with various women, and my mother said something like, "All cats look gray at night."

One of the children might have said something to the effect of "What does that mean?" Someone said that all women look the same in the dark and have their clothes off.

And I remember Michael said, "But I haven't seen the first one yet!"

I've raised three sons of my own, all grown men now. All of my stepchildren were all grown by the time they became my stepchildren. Probably the biggest influence I had with the stepchildren was bringing them together, and, at times, helping them and their father make a better relationship than they had previously. I could be a peacemaker in those relationships, because nobody was mad at me. I've enjoyed the step-grandchildren that I've acquired. Many have worked for me, and some have stayed with me, while looking for work.

I've always liked teenagers. I always felt better about my own children and other children when they began to talk. They tell the story that Rebecca Crisp asked her mother, "Now that I'm going to be in first grade at Fred Olds, can I go to see Doug? Does she like me now that I'm six?" Helen must have told her that she had to be very well behaved when she came to see me because I liked children after they got to be six or seven.

At the same time, so many children of friends and many other young people worked at Raleigh Creative Costumes, and that really was one of the real pleasures I had with the shop, watching kids grow up there. They came in at fourteen or fifteen, sometimes sixteen, to their first job, and seeing them blossom into adults has been very satisfying.

I wonder how single parents do it, because I think one of the saving graces when my sons were teenagers was the fact that, whichever one was mad at Ben, he would come to me or vice versa. It wasn't that they were pitting us against one another, but the other could talk without there being that basic anger in there. Also I felt very fortunate in that I had parents who were still young enough to be involved. I recall saying to Mother, "Could I send one of the children down?" And just for a few days out of the house for one of the children—it didn't matter which one—upset the balance of power.

Maybe that child really needed just to be considered extra special, and grandparents do that very well. My parents did not allow the children to do things that they knew we would not allow them to do. They expected to be respected and they expected good table manners or good manners in general. So they maintained the standards, but at the same time they would do special things with them. I felt sorry for people that did not have that opportunity to have grandparents that were that sort of involved.

As a mother, you spent a lot of time in the kitchen back then. As soon as you finished one meal, you were pretty much starting the next. You were thinking about what you'd use the leftovers for, so they don't look like leftovers, and how many people are you going to feed next time. My mother had a full-time job a good bit of the time when we lived in Raleigh, and off-and-on in Warrenton, but she also had full-time help in Warrenton. In Raleigh, she had Maggie about three days a week who did the cleaning and washing up, but not the cooking. I was fortunate to have had had some help, usually two to three days a week, to do whatever needed to be done, because you really cannot watch a child every minute.

I remember that were living in Sumter, in South Carolina. Right at the edge of our property, it became a swamp, and John was at the toddler age. You cannot go in and out of the house to hang clothes on the clothesline with a toddler and a basket of wet clothes, or a basket of dry clothes, and so I put a dog leash on the back of his little overalls and I hooked it to the clothesline. He could run back and forth on the clothesline while I was in and out of the house, getting clothes and putting them on the line or taking them off the line, but he couldn't wander out into the swamp and drown.

There are harnesses these days for little children, but it is awfully hard to get parents to use them. They are more common in Europe. I brought harnesses back for the Bennett twins, and I think the parents were sort of appalled. I always thought of it as a practical thing. Of course there, children are less likely to be going just from the house to the car, and from the car to a business, as we do here. There you will find people get off of the trolley or the bus and walk a good ways. Try walking yourself with your arm held up for ten minutes, as if holding your parent's hand as a child. You get tired. So if you put your child in a harness, you're not treating them like a little dog; you're being kind to them, I think.

But it doesn't hurt to have another pair of adult eyes there. That way you don't have to have the children right under your feet while you are cooking. They can be somewhere else in the house or in the yard, with somebody else helping to keep an eye on them.

And the help was always black, except in Austria I had white help. That was the first time I'd ever had white help, and at first that was a strange adjustment for me. You didn't have to be rich to have help. The cost of help was lower, very much lower. You paid them and you also paid their bus fare, and a certain amount that was not mentioned that was called "tote." Tote was the children's out-grown clothes, the leftovers from meals—the meal would be cooked and there would be enough also to send home that would feed the black family. At times, if the help were in a crisis, the employer might come in and go down to the courthouse and lend a hand.

Of course there were many families that were intertwined, black and white, and there were certain obligations back and forth on that. In my own family, there are certain Williams descendants that are considered black. Now, when we're talking about "intertwining," we're are not talking about intermarrying, but intercourse certainly—children from "the other side of the blanket."

You see more black and white couples now. I know that when I went to Ireland with the teenagers from my church, the first question I was asked by my hostess there was were there many integrated marriages, and my thought was black-white. Hers was Protestant-Catholic. Over here, that may be an issue for some, but it's still less of an issue than blacks and whites.

After Civil Rights, it became less common to have household help just because there were other jobs open to them, although it also hurt many of the teachers. With the integration of schools, many of these black teachers would be let go because the white teachers were there already, and they certainly were not going to lose their positions. The black teachers had to really work and prove themselves, and many of them did. At Frances Lacy school, I know when they had their first black principal—I think her name was Polk—parents were all upset. Then in about three years they were upset if they couldn't get their child into that school. That would have been in the late '60s, probably. She had proven herself in three years.

The Polks though have always been an educated family. They owned all of Method, which they had inherited from their Boylan ancestor, for whom Boylan Heights is named. And they still own a lot of the land over there in Method, the area over behind WRAL Studios.

Amanda Polk worked for me for a few years, and she and I had always had a close relationship. We'd sit around and talk. She came to my children's weddings, and I went to her children's weddings. We might not go to each other's church—not for a usual thing—but if it was a special occasion we might. Her grandson made Eagle Scout, and it was a big to-do. I was there too. I'm sure that it is a different relationship than I'd have with a white woman that I'd known that long, and yet it was a very close relationship and our children know this. There's no way that I know of to describe the difference. Yes, I have this knowledge that we came from different places, and yet we know each other as who we are.

Part II: Their Words

Chapter Sixteen
No Home Should Be Without One

Joel, Doug's oldest son, lives in Raleigh where he has been a freelance sculptor and writer for almost forty years. You can see some of his sculptures on joelhaasstudio.com or read his stories of the Haas family on his blog joelhaasstories.blogspot.com.

I was sitting in a repair shop with Mom some thirty years ago, and she was going on about some cousin's wedding. Being from Eastern North Carolina, we are related to everyone. Everybody in Eastern North Carolina is related to everybody, black and white. And she just hauled into it like I know who these people are, describing the wedding in detail. "...And Cousin So-And-So's bridesmaids were wearing this and that and the other. And the bride was wearing such-and-such, with the pearls, and so on..."

All of a sudden, a biker with a multi-colored mohawk, huge boots, keys rattling on down past

253

his knees, and a big leather jacket came walking in, and Mom didn't miss a beat. "That man needs more green on the back of his head..." and then just continued right on about the wedding.

It's summed up by Mom being an elder in the Presbyterian church and a judge at the drag queen beauty contest. Mom is certainly not a "little old lady" in her retirement. You would think of these ladies, almost ninety, reading Miss Marple, while I get, "Son, this is just a fascinatin' biography of Reinhold Niebuhr..."

Mom was never at loss for a story, which is what has made her a good salesman. I was reminded of this last year. We were visiting friends in Austria, the Seifs. There is a castle that we could see from the little village when we lived there called Kreuzenstein. Kreuzenstein Castle is unusual. The province of lower Austria is unusual in and of itself. It's about the size of the Research Triangle and has about 550 different castles and palaces, so there's one on every corner and people don't pay a lot of attention. But Kreuzenstein is one of those unusual castles that didn't actually exist. It was put together by an extremely wealthy mad baron living in the 1870s who bought six castles from around Europe, disassembled them, brought them to this lone hill in the Tullner Plane north of the Danube, and built them together. And they look like the absolute storybook castle.

She would take people over there for the tours, and Mom's understanding of German, if it didn't involve shopping for food or getting the fuse box replaced, was sometimes shaky. Nothing daunted. If Mom didn't know, Mom would make up the story. It got to the point that the tour guides knew my mother so well that, if there were Brits or Americans visiting that day, they simply shepherded them over to my mother, who would take them along with her guests—whoever was visiting from Raleigh—and take them along through the castle. And there was no question left unanswered, whether the answer was correct or not.

So it wasn't just my father who was a storyteller. In fact, I think my brothers and I get at least fifty percent of the creativity from my mother. And it's not just a matter of creativity. Even these days, how would you know if Mom were losing it? Because a normal conversation might be, "Son, I can't talk to you right now. There's a tiger at the door and I simply must get a moose on the bus to Jacksonville."

One time, Mom was in a frenzy. She had lost her business clothes and she was going to a costumer's convention. Well, the idea of Momma with business clothes was somewhat alien to me. "What are we looking for, Mom?"

"Well, I've got the silver lamé top hat and the cane, but I cannot find the silver lamé jumpsuit." She's obviously not going to interview at IBM.

There's always been that unselfconscious eccentricity and a fearlessness that's conveyed with that. I remember years ago I had come back to the United States. I must have been twenty-two at the time, and Mom and Dad were still in Austria. My mother mailed me a hollow chocolate rabbit for Easter, and I wrote Mom back that the rabbit had arrived, but that U.S. Customs had unfortunately investigated it for drugs because it was busted into a thousand pieces. Mom was furious.

Mom went down to the village post office and wanted to send a telegram. The village post office was the place where you went to use the telephone, you went to pay your water bill, your gas bill, your taxes, your car tag stuff if you actually owned a car, your dog license—whatever.

So my mother went down to the post office and sent a telegram to the White House in Washington, DC. This was the height of the Watergate hearings. Of course, she was sending it in English, so they were just copying it, letter for letter, and she sent, "Resign, you son of a bitch. You busted a child's Easter rabbit. Shameful!"

A few hours later, the gate doorbell rang. Mom wasn't back yet, so Dad answered it. It was the mailman, and he was very embarrassed. He showed Dad the telegram and said, "Of course we haven't mentioned it to anyone else in the village."

It was still a law on the books in Austria—and it still is, as a matter of fact—you cannot abuse or be rude to a public servant. It comes from the days of the monarchy. When you insulted a public officer, you insulted the Emperor himself. And that's a felony by the way.

The Austrians were very much in favor of Nixon. After all, they lived with the reality that the Soviets had a nuclear air base twenty-five miles from Vienna. Nixon was the guarantor of Austria and the Free World as far as they were concerned. Watergate? Well, hell, they'd lived through worse.

And of course, it's very embarrassing, man-to-man, that my father couldn't control his wife. You wouldn't want that sort of thing out in the village either.

Dad looked at the telegram, handed it back, and said, "Sign my name to it too."

We wound up in Austria because Dad had his first two novels sold to Simon & Schuster with paperback rights, and his share back in 1964 was $50,000, back when $50,000 was actually $50,000 dollars. And so, he announced that we were going to move someplace that we had never been and didn't speak the language, which, except for his service in the Philippines in the Second World War, was for the rest of us anywhere, speaking anything. A few months later we wound up in a little farming village three hundred meters from the Vienna woods.

The first day we were there, they were re-paving *Schubert-gasse* where we had rented a house, and this was steep road. It was the first time we had seen a sidewalk with handrails. And the fact is the Austrians weren't going to be over-concerned with putting in a base, so each Spring the asphalt slid down, which was all right because it was a Socialist country and they needed the employment. Nobody had cars. There was only one family on the entire street that had a car. We would later become the second family who had a car on the street. They were just going to pave right on over the driveway entrance. Dad wasn't there. We didn't speak any German at the time. And Mom said, "We may just have to sit down, all of us. The three of you little boys will just sit there, and we will sway back and forth and sing *We Shall Overcome.*"

You Broads

The next day my brothers were dumped in a grammar school down the mountainside, and the day after that, Mom and I walked to Klosterneuburg, which was the next town up the cobblestone Roman way. The Romans had laid this road down and it had been made to Roman specifications, wide enough for a dead man on a chariot. It was not designed for two-way traffic of cars. You had to keep that in mind and know that sometimes even jumping up onto the sidewalk was no sure defense against getting hit.

We walked on to the next village, which was about two and a half miles. I remember it was a November day, and the sky was slate gray and overcast. There was a lady coming up the street, steaming up the hill like a ship in heavy seas, and she had both hands full with shopping bags because of course you'd bring bags to the store. You would go daily. None of them had refrigerators so you'd have to go daily. How are you going to keep anything cold? She had her wool coat on and her little hat with a feather, and she no more really expected to meet an American woman than she expected to meet pink Martians. This was not a touristy area of Austria. I mean, the Russians left because it just really wasn't worth it.

My mother stopped her and accosted her, and at this point things go off the track. Mom was wearing this green suede full-length coat, nice shoes—an American lady. You have to remember that, far and away, Americans were the richest people in the world at the time, and Mom confused the word for "school" with the word for "shoes." So she stopped this woman and demanded shoes for her child. I was standing there, a thirteen-year old American kid who was certainly dressed better than any child in the town. And of course this woman thinks, "Ok, I have been walking along, minding my own business, coming back from the bakery, and I encounter an American woman who demands shoes for her son, who's perfectly well-shod. She might be psychotically dangerous. But being Americans there would be a fearful fuss if anything were to happen to them, and I'd be to blame."

She walked a mile and a half down the street with us again to the town square and took us into a shoe store, where, thanks be to God, one of the clerks spoke English to explain that we had been standing right in front of the school, actually. And this school—which is now a very modern building and completely different to the one I went to—was a former residence of the Von Trapp family, one of their *pied a terre* in Vienna. It was an old pile, still painted Habsburg yellow, with an enormous profile of *Der Altefranzel*—which is Viennese for "Old Francis," Franz Josef, who was the Emperor—in the middle. The seal of the Emperor was all over the place. Despite the Nazis, despite the Church, despite the Russians, most things were Habsburg yellow and most things still had the seal of Franz Josef. To one side of the seal was a door with the fancy *fraktur* writing, *knaben*, the German word for boys, and on the other end of the building, *mädchen*. Boys and girls went in separate doors. We didn't know what door to go in, but we evidently went in the right one.

We walked down the halls, wide wooden halls and huge ceilings with nobody there. Finally, we encountered someone who looked like Boris Karloff, about 6'4", impeccably dressed, white hair. It turns out, he was the school principal, but he did not speak English. He took us to his office. When Boris Karloff tells you to come to his office, you go, and he called someone else. Evidently the English teacher was summoned. Matters were explained and a few forms filled out. There was some confusion because the German word for Protestant is "*evangelisch*," which we would interpret as Evangelistic, which Presbyterians from Raleigh certainly were not. Ninety-eight percent of Austrians being Catholics, the word never came up much.

The principal went along with us and we went down that long hall again and came to a huge wooden door with "3A" written on it, and he banged on the door. We heard a shuffle all of a sudden, the chairs coming out and being pushed aside. It was a whole room of boys standing at attention. They were wearing knee-high leather knickers and green wool jackets, not because that's the uniform but because that's something that's warm and inexpensive and something that was generally handed down several generations because it really lasted. They were sitting two to the wooden desk with pen inkwell sort of thing and, again, everyone was standing to attention as was the teacher, who I believe was the math teacher at the time.

The principal came in, kind of barked something in German, and one of the boys at the back came to more attention and said, "I am from Kritzendorf too. My name is Alfred."

Well, evidently Alfred had been told, "Take care of the American. Sponsor him. Don't let anyone beat him up." Alfred and I became very good friends. We sat in the back together.

But that was Mom's encounter with the first
day of school. "Shoes and school. Never confuse
those again."

Another attribute of my mom's, and I think my
father's as well—this was a professional thing for
Dad, his being able to get along with anybody and
interview anybody—but my mother had the
special ability to float and be friends with all sorts
of factions. You certainly saw that in the theater
community in Raleigh. You just couldn't have
these people at the same party but every one of
them considered Mom their best friend. And in a
village like Kritzendorf, which had existed for
hundreds of years, and given the history of
Austria in the last fifty years, everyone in the
village knew who had sent whose dad or uncle to
which concentration camp. There were people who
did not speak to each other for reasons much more
than just ego over the stage. And somehow, Mom
picked up on all that and just managed to float.
There were just certain families that you didn't
have over to the same *soiree*. But she was great
friends with all of them.

With Dad, he was interviewing everybody, and
my mother and father together—and I know I had
a gallery dealer once who pointed out that I had
picked up this trait as well—they collected

eccentrics. If there were an eccentric within fifty miles...

One time in 1972 or 1971, there was one guy in Austria who had lived up in the mountains like a German of 2000 B.C., his special dispensation from the state of Lower Austria, to hunt deer with a bronze bow and arrow. And he lived in a hut, etcetera, and raised goats. He was a living museum. He had had lost his mind. He was a machine gun sergeant in Yugoslavia in the Second World War, and Yugoslavia was at least as vicious if not more so than Russia. And he came out of the war a complete pacifist and convinced that there would be world peace if everyone went back to their ancient folkways. He was the man who taught me how to fence with a broadsword, and he was delighted I would wear blue jeans—that was my folk costume. If I wore *lederhosen*, that was just lame. That was not my folk costume and I would be unhappy. And it just infuriated him when Austrians would wear blue jeans to visit him. So of course, he's worked into one of Dad's books.

We hired a maid, Frau Kainrat, and she was the first white maid any of us had ever seen. You couldn't find a black maid in Austria. Mom didn't know how to relate with her. She had to sort of feel her way. To some extent, my parents did all the social things that they had been raised with. I remember one time they sent her to the opera to see *Madame Butterfly*. I don't think Frau Kainrat was used to that. Years later, when my grandparents visited, Frau Kainrat told my mother that she was so impressed with my grandfather. She used the word "gentleman," which when it's used in German has a much more exalted connotation. "He takes his hat off even when he speaks to *me*."

And Mom went about making friends there, becoming engaged in the customs and taking part in them, and Mom and Dad both made friends very quickly, I think Mom even more quickly because she was right there with the kids. We also got very lucky in that the Bauer family—the current generation of Seifs, their grandmother Bauer was the head of the grammar school at the bottom of the mountain. And Frau Bauer spoke English well and introduced my mother to several people.

I remember in Austria one time Helmut Seif telling my father that Dad's politics were nearly Communist but he was almost a Nazi with his family. And being a conservative guy, my dad did not have beards or pierced ears or long hair. He looked like a factory foreman. Dad would be the type of guy to say, "All right. Cut your hair. Put on a tie. We're going to go downtown to protest."

My mother and father were both on board about how children were raised. And it was old fashioned by modern standards. We always said, "Yes, Sir" and "No, Sir," "Yes, Ma'am" and "No, Ma'am." You asked, "May I be excused from the table?" You said grace before supper—the whole bit. And Dad and Mom, and my grandparents for that matter, would say, "Do you want me to take off my belt?" Or I remember my grandmother making me go out and pick out the switch. And as you can tell, we're not badly distorted felons for having endured corporal punishment.

When they came back from Austria in 1975, Mom and Dad didn't have kids at the house anymore, so Mom and Sue Federici decided they would start a costume business, and that first Halloween they started basically at the dining room table of 2818 Bedford Avenue. And they did really well. So the following year, they moved into Sue Federici's mother-in-law's basement and had a bigger area. Then they rented a house over on West Johnson Street that is no longer there. There's a big apartment building there now. It was a little house and they turned it into a costume shop.

You Broads

At the time, I was running a little hobby shop about a block and a half away called The Armoury—military miniatures. I had models and books of military histories. In fact, I've got a bunch of figures that I've still got to get rid of and sort. Becoming a sculptor, my lead into things was I knew the people who were model collectors or manufacturers of toy soldiers and all sorts of miniatures. Somebody has to make the original for them to make the models. I'm a really good sculptor now because, after doing about a thousand of them, you learn about how the head bone is connected to the neck bone.

So anyway, Dad was working on *House of Christina*, and it was behind schedule, as all of Dad's major books were. Dad sent in a manuscript in 1976 and two days later collapsed of a heart attack. He didn't die but he was at Western Wake Hospital, which back then was in Apex and had eight beds. I was about to call his Western paperback publisher and see about writing a couple paperbacks to get some cash in quick to pay bills while Dad was in the hospital. I had already started to write some paperbacks for Dad in a series. I was twenty-six.

Peter Schwade, the head editor at Simon & Schuster called and he said, "I understand from Bill Reese," that was Dad's agent, "that you're the only person Ben has talked to about editing this book."

I said, "Yeah, but I've got to see about writing some paperbacks or something because I need to get some cash in here."

He said, "Kid, how much cash do you need?"

I said, "Five thousand dollars."

He said, "I'll wire it to you tomorrow. We're not publishing *War and Peace* this season. Forty thousand words need to come out of that book." So yours truly, with Larry Bliss and Russell Hermon, the three of us edited *The House of Christina*. I would do the original cut. Larry would do the copy-editing and Russell would do what Larry and I didn't do.

The doctors figured out that Dad would have another heart-attack if they didn't give him a pencil and paper. From my point-of-view, that was a really bad mistake because Dad was on all the drugs what were illegal if you're not at the hospital, and he decided he was going to re-write the whole damn book in long-hand between the lines. So I would bring him out edited versions to see, and he would go on about how I was ruining things and what was screwed up about it, and he would give me his edits. I would go home, not even look at his edits, and drop them in the trash can. Mom already had a bourbon and water ready in the middle of the table for me and would not say anything. We got forty thousand words out of that, and Dad's share of that book was four hundred thousand dollars. And you know what I thought? I was so relieved, because if he hadn't made a lot of money out of that, I had screwed up.

The following year when Dad died, I remember Jeanie and I had gone over to Raleigh Creative Costumes on Bedford Avenue because the washing machine we had broke and we were going to use Mom's. It was three days before Halloween, and nobody else was there. Dad had gone up to New York. The Literary Guild was having a dinner for authors. Dad was having a hassle with his Westerns publisher. They were in a copyright dispute.

I was standing in the hall and the phone rang, and I remember saying to Jeanie, "That's Bill Reese, calling from New York." I don't know why I said it. I picked up the phone and it was.

And Bill told me, "I have awful, awful news for you." He said, "You father has died."

My first reaction was, "What? In a foreign land?"

And Bill said he was supposed to meet Dad at the Algonquin Bar. Dad never showed.

I went down to West Johnson Street, and the first person I talked to was Dottie Streb and

Spragh Silver—good friends of my parents and they were a block up the street. Spragh, the first thing he did was he got his Jack Daniels. He poured a triple and said, "Take this on down to your momma. I'm walking with you."

Mom had made a huge amount of money that year at the shop, compared to anything she had ever seen. And she said she would have loved to have shared that with him.

Then she married Willard in 1981, and I've got to say, the step-siblings are great and Willard was great. He was completely different from my old man. The joke was that Mom had married a genius of the nineteenth century and then she married a genius of the twenty-first century. The guy had two doctorates, one in analytical chemistry and the other in nuclear physics. He invented what is basically the scientific equivalent of the wheel for astronomers, the mass spectrometer that can go into space—so if you're the Hubble telescope, you better have one of those things.

The cool thing about Willard was, he did not understand a thing that I or my brothers did, but he understood it was our passion, and he understood that because his comment to us was, "Well, you know, I've never 'worked' a day in my life either," because he was into physics and stuff like that.

Plus, I owe Becky Hanner and Ward Bennett big time because they had the grandchildren. I remember Mom took my nephew Logan—who is now in his mid-thirties and has got two kids and is a respectable businessman—when Logan was thirteen, she took him on his European tour to give him some polish. I remember her coming back, "Well, he knows how to order drinks at the interval at the West End..." Her definition of polish; he can order Oma's drinks.

I mean, Mom is interesting. In January of 2017 she had me come over and said, "Son, would you help me put these Christmas glasses away on the top shelf?"

I get up on the step stool, and the top shelf is full. I said, "Mom, I don't think we can put them on this shelf."

"Then let's put them on the shelf over the refrigerator."

I take the step stool over and I get up, and on top of the refrigerator is this big box that says, "jive." So I pass it down and I say, "Momma, what's in the 'jive' box?"

"Oh, that is a life-sized gelatin mold of the Queen of England's head. Your brother had one at his party, and I liked it so much, so he sent me one."

I said, "Well, no home should be without one." That's what Dad used to say when Mom would bring in something a little off-the-wall. No home should be without one. That was my immediate response. It was bright pink.

Mom was asked to be the Queen of England. One of her neighbors on the *Rue Sans Familie* is English, and for his birthday he was going to get a visit from the Queen. I think David Serxner dressed her. And then the gelatin mold I think was fill with crab jelly or some sort of savory gelatin. I've got pictures of Mom conferring knighthood on whole swaths of people.

So if you ever need a gelatin mold of the Queen of England's head, that's one of the nice things about Momma. You don't have to go buy one yourself. You know where it is. The question would be, does Mom know where it is?

One time I remember going up to Cherry Hill. Mom's family is from the Warrenton area, and Cherry Hill is an exact replica of Mom's ancestral place, Buxton Place, which is a mile down the road from Cherry Hill, both built by the same architect, builders, etcetera. And Cousin Edgar Thornton lived there along with his sister, and he left the house to a private non-profit he'd set up and they'd have classical music concerts there a couple of times a year. And Mom's been on the board and of course would go up there occasionally. It's the real thing. The first time I walked in there, the drapes, you know, they had been put up in 1859 and they had not been taken down or moved since. This was normal living as far as I was concerned. You walked in and the place had been outfitted in 1859 and Cousin Edgar had seen no reason to change the furniture or anything. He had brought in some modern books when he retired from New York, where he was an art critic.

So we're going to go up to one of the concerts, and Mom says, "Let's pack a picnic and we will have lunch at the grave of Annie Lee." That was the daughter of General Robert E. Lee who died while in refuge in Warrenton in 1864.

At this time when you drove across the Warren County line, I mean, you entered a different time and space. Warrenton was 2,000 people. It had shrunk since "the War" and still supported six hardware stores, one of whom was run by a guy who was a dead ringer for Truman Capote. We're going along there and we're driving in Warren County.

"Momma, where is Annie Lee's grave?"

"Well, I don't rightly remember, but it is around here somewhere."

"Can you picnic at Annie Lee's grave? Have they got picnic tables there or something?"

"Well, I don't know. It's been decades since I've been there."

"It could be grown over, for all you know!"

"Well, I don't know where it is. It's just around here somewhere…"

I said, "Why don't we just drive on to Cherry Hill and have a picnic there."

"Because you're not allowed to drink alcohol on the grounds of Cherry Hill. Cousin Edgar wrote that into his will."

"Cousin Edgar drank like a fish! What the hell are we talking about?"

And she said, "Well, he was concerned—see, we make our money by renting it out for wedding receptions, and so on—that some drunk would drop his cigarette there and burn the place down."

I say, "Ok." So, fine, we go driving into Inez. Inez is a wide spot in the road south of Warrenton. You can tell you're in Inez because the bears are slightly more urbane.

Next door to Cherry Hill is the Methodist church. It's two in the afternoon on Sunday. There's nobody there, so we drive into the parking lot of the Methodist church. I get out to open the trunk for the picnic basket. I open the trunk, and there is no picnic basket there but there are a dozen bright red top hats with devil horns on them and eight submachine guns. No home should be without one. And apparently everyone in Inez will get one.

Eventually I clear all this away and find there is a picnic basket there. There are several bottles of wine. And Pam gets Mom settled on the steps of the Methodist church, and we uncork a bottle of wine and start having our picnic. Three people drive up. I'm thinking they're Methodists; they're gonna chase us off. No, they're lost. You can't get lost in Inez. It turns out they are looking for one of only three people I know in Warren County, and I send them on
their way.

Chapter Seventeen
A Very Willful Child

Doug's son Michael lives in England with his husband Kevin Bell. After completing his PhD, he now co-chairs the exil.arte Center, a research unit based at Vienna's University of Music and Performing Arts that repatriates the musical estates of former refugees fleeing the Third Reich.

Probably born to another generation, my mother would not have chosen to be a mother, first and foremost, but she was certainly a very conscientious mother. She was very affectionate, very demonstrably affectionate. She was sympathetic. She was kind. She could also be very angry.

But one of the things that I think I'm most grateful to her for is that, just as generations ago parents might decide who you get married to, in my generation parents had a very clear idea of what you had to do in order to get on in life, whether this was to become a lawyer or a doctor or accountant or whatever. You had to go and get an education and get the best grades and achieve and be compliant to all of society's demands. And just as in due course society changed to say, "No, parents will not decide who you get married to. You get married for love. You get married to whom you want to get married to," well my mother believed the same applied to work. You couldn't be happy unless you were actually doing something that you really loved. And her view was you will be happier in life earning less but doing something you love than earning a lot and doing something that you just can't wait to stop doing, because what are you going to do with the money? Can the money buy you the sense of fulfillment that doing a job you love would be able to provide?

And so I think we were encouraged to do that by her and by the very example of my dad. Today I notice, particularly because of technology, people have no demarcations between work and free time. In those days, at five o'clock you were no longer an employee. You were a dad. And in our family that was never the case because he was never employed by anybody and he worked at home, largely at home, although he had an office somewhere. So what he did and who he was were very much the same thing. Everybody else's daddy, they worked in an office or they did this or they did that, and when the buzzer sounded, they stopped and they became who they really were. We grew up with this idea that you were what you did.

I had no sense of how much or how little money there was in the family. Like all families, there were probably times of affluence and times of less affluence, and there were shouting matches between them, which I do remember, which concerned money. But I don't remember feeling as if we were deprived. I always felt as if we got fantastic Christmas presents. We got fantastic birthday presents. From a material point of view, there was very little our parents denied us. But oddly enough, they encouraged us somehow to want things that were probably beneficial to us as well. They encouraged interests in us.

One day I announced I wanted a pipe organ for Christmas. And I saw these great big, multi-keyboard organs for sale in department stores. Well those cost tens of thousands of dollars. There was no way on Earth my parents could afford that sort of thing, nor was there any room in the house. It would have been insane to have indulged me in that. So they bought me the complete works of Bach on recording, and it was a much better present. I was much happier with it. And it was the sort of kind of lateral thinking that my parents always employed that kept us happy within our material needs while making sure our spiritual and intellectual needs were also being met.

My mother came from what I would call *nouveau pauvre*, and Dad's family was of very mixed background, including a healthy dose of German Jewish immigrant, and that caused a certain amount of disquiet within her family.

She never has gone into the specifics of why they disapproved of her marrying Dad, except that he wasn't a near relative, and everyone else in that part of the world married their third or fourth cousins, at least within a certain social stratum. So her very act of marrying this guy who didn't have a traditional Eastern North Carolina surname, and whose background was equally dubious, was a break in some ways from her traditional upbringing.

She didn't have a debutante party. She went to schools and got thrown out of schools for various issues. But on the other hand, she could be amazingly conventional and remains amazingly conventional. You can tell when I haven't got a tie on and she thinks I should have a tie on. She may not say anything but you can feel her biting her tongue. And if I say, "Do I need to wear a tie for this?" probably the closest she will come to saying, nowadays, "Yes, you have to put on a tie," is, "Well there will be a lot of people there wearing ties..."

A Very Willful Child

I was flabbergasted when I discovered the attitude of my grandparents to my parents' marriage, because my grandparents were the most loving, attentive, constructive, generous people you could imagine. I loved being at my grandparents' place. I never was in a position to ask them directly how they could have objected to my mother marrying my dad. In retrospect, you can probably see that their objections were on-the-mark because there was a cultural clash between them, things that are now manifest in us, which would have not been the case had she married another Henderson or another Crawford or another Taylor.

By default, we stopped being WASPs. We're not quite Anglo-Saxon Protestants anymore. You come with a German, partially-Jewish name like Haas and you exit the WASP enclave. You are no longer part of "Old America." You are part of "Immigrant America." And I think Immigrant America has a different relationship to America. Immigrant America has a hyphen attached to it. You're a German-American. You're a Jewish-American. And that hyphen definition, what your self-identity is, is probably what led Dad to want to go to Austria. This whole inability unquestioningly to accept the Anglo-Saxon definition of who we are is the legacy that comes from marrying somebody who is not another Eastern North Carolina "First Family of Virginia."

By marrying Dad, my mother inevitably was thrown in a world that was in many ways very foreign to her. She's a bright woman. She reads a lot, and when she accompanied my dad, who was obviously a massively literate individual and moved in literary circles, she could hold her own. But moving in literary circles is not what Southern Belles tend to do. So you have this mixture of moving in literary circles on the one hand—lots of alcohol, late nights, cigarettes—and then still feeling like if you go to church on Sunday, you must wear a tie.

You have to remember, she grew up at a time when you just rarely met somebody from out of the state, let alone out of thencountry. So the world was a far more provincial place in her childhood. The world was a far more enclosed, cocooned place, and she was unique or daring in her youth for wanting to break out of that. So perhaps marrying Dad was just an act of demonstration of how she was not going to carry on just living in this Southern Belle cocoon that had been pre-ordained for her.

Now, I was born in Charlotte, NC, in 1954. I'm the middle of the three sons. My first memories are of Sumter, SC, and the swamp in the back yard. Of course the front of the house was just nothing but a sand pit. It was a veritable desert, and it must have been hell on earth for my mother.

In Sumter in the '50s, mothers could devolve a lot of the day-to-day baby care to local black women. Daily there was at least one if not two who took care of us. I suppose probably they were just teenage girls, but to me they looked grown up. And I remember these black women being incredibly friendly and also sympathetic and generous, and all these things. I just remember being surrounded by a lot of nice, good people. And of course when you are surrounded by nice, good people you grow up thinking everybody is like that.

I remember the magic and the happiness of playing in Sumter and thinking Sumter was great, picking up lizards and toads and shoving them into my pocket and playing with them. Today if I see a lizard and I try to pick it up, or approach a toad or a frog, they hop away. But as a child, I remember just walking to them and picking them up. Maybe that's what it takes, no sort of hesitation. My mom said she got to the point where she'd have to empty my pockets before she put them in the washing machine.

Her Words

One time I came in walking in from the swamp with two enormous frogs underneath my arms. My new friends, they were. They were splayed with their back legs dangling and their front legs over my forearms, and I tried to show one to Mom. Of course she wasn't thrilled. And at that moment, the frogs began ejecting spawn. Everybody screamed, including me. I threw the frogs up in the air, and frog spawn went in all directions.

To me these are magical memories. To my mother, these are probably absolutely horrifying.

My dad may have encouraged her to move in certain social circles there, but they were pretty restrictive social circles. There was an Air Force base there. I think the only people out there were military wives. She was young enough to adjust, and she's interested in other people, so even if she's sitting around with a bunch of plastic "Stepford Wives," she probably could find enough in common to make her existence at least tolerable.

Obviously, her return to Raleigh must have been an enormous relief for her, but I was suddenly deprived of this perfect playground. Plus it happened to coincide exactly with the time when they shipped me off to school as well. I never went to school in Sumter. I remember they sent me to Ravenscroft School, and this teacher stood in front of the class and said things, and I remember just bringing down the shutters, saying, "I don't like this and I'm not going to participate." And the shutters basically stayed down until I left school sixteen years later. I hated Raleigh. I just hated it.

Even as a child, I was fanatical about classical music. This was weird in North Carolina. And this incredible, all absorbing fascination with music woken in me was incompatible with everything in Raleigh. Even being sent to good public schools, which we had, there were no facilities for dealing with things that were generally important to me. And the result is that the things that were important to everybody else were not important to me.

So I had a combination of whammies. I had the whammy of being gay—probably not realizing I was gay at that point but realizing I was different—and being made aware of the fact that I was different in that I was aware of something that all of the other guys were not interested in.

It wasn't just a question of "I don't like sports." There were plenty of other people who felt school sports were a complete waste of time, but nobody was there to convince me the academic subjects were adjuncts to what I was really interested in. No one could draw the relationship between being good in history or mathematics in order to add to your enthusiasm of music. And they saw the reason I wasn't excelling in their courses as a kind of act of rebellion. They always put me in streamed classes, very high classes, top classes, but I always did very badly. I think that, by the time I left Broughton, I had failed every single course, including Germain. And I spoke German as well as the teacher.

The teacher said, "German is not a class for someone who speaks the language. The way we teach it is different than the way you would speak it." For example, an exam question would be, "Can you name the prepositions that determine both dative and accusative case? How many are there?" Well if I speak German, I use the prepositions correctly, but to this day I could never list the prepositions that are sometimes accusative and sometimes dative.

And of course I was lazy. They would say, "This is your translation exercise for tomorrow," and it would be some stupid little story that wasn't inspiring enough for me to be able to read. I wouldn't bother. Then they would give me the vocabulary list, and if I listed synonyms instead of the words that were listed at the end of the chapter... So I failed everything.

A Very Willful Child

It was years later that I realized there were many missed opportunities there. It's not Raleigh's fault, but for that reason, I don't consider Raleigh home.

I certainly consider Vienna much more home. It was a place where I found plenty of guys, straight and gay, who shared my interests right down to a "T," where a love of classical music was not instantly a rainbow flag stuck in your back pocket. It was perfectly normal of local culture. And I loved speaking German. I speak German without any accent. No one asks me where I come from when I speak German. So it's a different existence and I feel happiest there.

But I've spent the majority of my life based in the UK now, so the UK is very much home for me, but it's a different type of home. It's the home of my adult life. It's not the home of my childhood or my youth.

When I first moved to the UK, I hated it. I thought London an absolute pit. I really didn't like it at all. The toilets didn't flush. The first bit of advice I got in London was, when you travel on the Underground, travel in the smoking carriage so you don't have to smell the other people. And the meanness of the people, the stinginess of the people, and the hypocrisy of the people was just staggering.

But it was all still post-war back in those days, and then all of a sudden the country played catch-up, and now when I walk through London I think, this is an amazing city. There's not a bit of graffiti or litter. It's clean. It's tidy. It's spectacularly restored. The parks are clean and green. And, ok, the weather isn't great, but everything else in the city is absolutely beautiful and you can understand why tourists want to go there. The buildings are gleaming and new and high, and the roads are paved, and the people have good teeth. It wasn't that way when I first arrived.

When I met Kevin, that's when I decided I wanted to buy the flat in London. Before then, I was ready to get out of the place. I had just had my nose full. But I met Kevin, and I felt all of a sudden that, right, well, I'm prepared to take root here.

I was married, and I left my wife. I married my wife at the age of twenty-three, and at that age you're just about prepared to go to bed with anybody who is prepared to go to bed with you. Only later do you realize this might or might not be the gender you prefer to sleep with.

The longer we were married, the clearer it was to me that heterosexuality was not natural to me. It was unnatural to me. And we lived at a time when a woman's sexual needs were just the same as a man's sexual needs. So a woman who then finds that her husband or her partner is obviously not able to do more than just the most fundamental, basic, limited amount that is expected, when her own needs are far greater than that, also then realizes that this is not a marriage where the intimacy is going to be great. And I think people demand a certain intimacy in the solidifying of a relationship together.

I came out to her quite soon. I told her early on that I was attracted to men, but it didn't appear to have much effect on our own married life, as we said euphemistically, except that as we became more and more sophisticated in what we wanted and what we needed and what we read and how we felt. This was the days before Internet porn, obviously, so you would pick up a book called *The Joy of Sex*, and she'd be looking at it going, "Wow!" And I'd be looking at it going, "Ugh!" So it was quite clear that this was a relationship that was never going to work.

Eventually, I did meet Kevin, and Kevin and I formed a very close relationship, and then it was very clear that he and I were a couple. And that was when I felt like, *Kevin is my family now. If I am rejected by my own family, well I have Kevin and that's important to me now.* That was the risk I took.

Her Words

My mother had agreed to facilitate a loan for me to buy my first property in England, which she didn't even want me to do. She didn't like me being in England. She didn't like England, and I can't blame her. Her first trip to London was in the early '60s and it was desperate, absolutely desperate. Her opinion was, "This place is a hole and my son has no business being here."

I told her I wanted to buy a flat in England, in London. You couldn't rent a place very easily in those days. And what you could rent, you didn't want to live in. The place that I had rented with Leslie my wife was still war damaged. You couldn't shut windows because of the damage. You had no central heating. We had to put a shower in. We had to put a toilet in.

So she wasn't favorably inclined to my life choices and she had agreed, reluctantly, to stump up a loan. She made her financial advisor draw up a contract with interest repayments and everything, and when I told her about Kevin, she withdrew the deal. She took it all back. "My son does not do this to me."

It fell into the same category of wearing a tie to church on Sunday. She thought this was an active act of rebellion from me, willful. And I had always been a "willful child." She knew that I'd smoked some dope and other these things that she knew I had done as a kind of act of rebellion. And she just decided that my coming out was just another act of rebellion.

You have to put into context what the attitude was towards gay people in those days. They were friendly with a gay couple, Harry and Art. And the first time we had them around for dinner, I remember my parents talking to me, and saying, "Sometimes when little boys grow up in unhappy families and they have no daddy, they don't grow up having healthy relationships with women but then grow up falling in love with other little boys."

This was her spin on why people turned gay, a little bit of half-baked Freudian popular psychology that she would have picked up in *The New Yorker* or something, and this was the liberal point of view in the '50s and '60s. So my mother seeing homosexuality as an unappealing but inevitable mental illness in some people was about as Liberal as she was prepared to go at about the point.

In fact, as the reality of me being gay slowly began to dawn on her, her first question was, "I don't remember you having a closer relationship with me than you did with your dad."

And I said, "Well, I didn't." I remember expecting and giving and taking different things from different parents, in equal measure. So there was no imbalance in the relationships, not at all. In fact, I think my parents were scrupulous about showing no favoritism and being equally involved in what they contributed to our upbringing.

Plus, she worked in the theater and she worked in costumes, and all the gays that she knew were the ones coming in to rent feather boas from her to go to drag balls, who were not necessarily representative of gay men. Back in those days, people would say, "I can tell who's gay at a hundred paces." Well, yeah, if somebody happens to swish down the street, you can say, "He's gay." You just don't to see the other twenty who have walked past you who look like everybody else.

So, the other question she asked me was, "Do you want to dress up in women's clothes?" That came very, very quickly.

And I said, "No."

My mother actually rejected me. She sort of wanted to stop all further communications, stop all transactions, absolutely stop everything. She wanted to have nothing more to do with me.

I was thirty. This was 1985. She was married to Willard at the time, and Willard was of course the same age as her father, and Willard's views were at least as Right Wing as her father. She knew Willard hated "homos." And she knew that she would never be able to introduce Kevin to Willard. Even when she did, I don't think it was ever clear to Willard who Kevin was.

This state of "he is no longer my son, I want nothing more to do with him" lasted about seventy-two hours. It was eventually changed by Dottie Streb's intervention. Dottie Streb is also a distant relative of my mother. I don't know in what respect. In that part of North Carolina, everybody is related to everybody, like I said. She was a very close friend even from childhood days, a little bit younger than my mum, I think. She was part of a group of friends that my dad and my mother hung out with, and she lived close by on Shepherd Street.

But Dottie was a hell of a lot more unbuttoned than my mother. She went duck hunting and she was fascinated by guns. She was actually a quite shocking individual, a full-on, heavy-duty, horse-riding, cigar-smoking Southern belle who drank a lot and smoke a lot and worked hard and ran a very successful business. I think she was an insurance broker or something.

But she was a big character in my mother's life, one of the close friends of my mother, and her son Raymond Streb was just another one of the adopted sons my mother took care of. Dottie was one of the rare women who ran a full-time business at that time, so Raymond would often come home and there was nobody there, nobody to cook for him, nobody to take care of him. So he'd just wander over to our house, which was two or three blocks down the road.

Dottie must have had some very long, deep, searching heart-to-hearts with my mother over those three days because she then came around, a bit like my grandparents with her and Ben. She eventually came around and came to be very fond of Kevin and now supports any number of gay causes. And I'm delighted that she does. And of course she knows more about it now. She knows that not all gay men are like the ones who come and rent feather boas from the shop. And gay men are a bit more visible than they were before. They're more in the media. They're more on television. They're more on film. She can see that's closer to how I and Kevin live than, say, *The Boys in the Band*, which was the only film at that point that had dealt with that kind of thing.

But at the time, it was not seemly to be gay. It's not done. It's not proper. The girl has left Warrenton long ago, but this is the Warrenton in the girl. And when it's not malevolent, as I found it was in the question of my sexuality, it is quite charming in other ways.

A Very Willful Child

She not only expects you to hold the door for people. She expects you to hold the chair for people. She expects you to say "Please" and "Thank you," and to introduce yourself when you walk into a room, all sorts of things which just add to the general civility of society. And, mercifully, I think some of that has washed off onto all of us.

Doug related her own memory of this moment in her relationship with Michael.

Michael came over I guess when either my mother or my father died, and at that point he came out to Dottie Streb and also to Gert Bliss. And they said, "Don't come out to Doug right now. She's got too much on her plate. She's just gotten married to Willard. She is establishing a new marriage. Just wait until things settled down." So he did not come out to me until after Willard died.

We were sitting on the back screened porch, back there on St. Mary's Street, talking about his life and I said, "I hope you meet another nice girl and fall in love again."

And he said, "Well, I have met somebody, but it's a he and not a she."

I was surprised because, of all the boys, Mike had dated the most variety of girls. And they all drooled over him. Getting the mail for him was like you were going to tear all the stamps off for a box of stamp collections, because they came from all over the world. See, he was going to the music school in Austria and students were there from all over the world. And he brought several girls home. Some he dated several times, some only once or twice. I remember we went to a ski resort one Easter and this girl from Thailand went there too to be near him. Ben said, "Mike is smeared with musk."

So I was somewhat shocked. I said, "I hope you'll be very happy." And he had been, of course.

It took me a while to digest this and think about it. I talked to Gert and I talked to Dottie about it a bit. I always thought that the gal he had married was a strange choice. She just didn't seem to have the spark of life that all the girls he'd usually dated had. She was not a musician, nor was she a party girl. She was into social justice. I think she was a social worker.

They met at St. Ninian's. This was a center in Scotland for Presbyterians, and he was working there because he wasn't really sure what he wanted to do. He knew he didn't want to be a concert pianist, but music was the main thing he had been trained for. So he had been singing in the choir of the Scottish Presbyterian church in Austria, which was an English language church, and the minister said, "Why don't you go up to St. Ninian's for a year as a volunteer and gets your thoughts together." A lot of people did that. And when he got there he met a girl who frankly looked so much like him that in the photographs you have to say, "Which is which?"

Mike had met Kevin and was living with Kevin, but he hadn't told me they were together. Kevin was just one of many friends he might mention in a letter.

So I had to give this some thought and to ask, "Is he happy?" This is a hard life for anybody, but right then particularly to admit you were gay was really a hard life. Mike later told me he dated all those girls to see if maybe he wasn't really gay.

The apartment they have now is very frankly a penthouse. I mean, it could be a movie set. It has a long glass front, two living rooms, and a dining room, all facing the Thames with floor-to-ceiling windows, and then that opens onto a thousand square-foot rooftop garden. They have the same gardener who does the Prince of Wales' garden.

And Mike and Kevin have been together for a long time now and definitely seem to be very happy.

Her Words

Chapter Eighteen
Mr. President

John, Doug's youngest son, splits his time between New York and California, working as a consultant helping universities develop and implement long-range strategies for their technology. Previously, John directed and stage-managed operas.

With Mom, I have long since understood that I only see one part of what is a very active and rich life. I remember asking Mom about how she read, and she said, "Well, when I'm in the living room, I read this book. When I'm in the bathroom I read that book. And when I'm in the car, I read that book."

And I said, "In the car?"

She said, "Yes, well, you know, when I'm stopped at a stoplight or there's a train going along Dan Allen Drive, I just need something that I can read some short pieces from, so I carry a copy of *Canterbury Tales* along with me." And she's had a copy of *Canterbury Tales* in her glove compartment forever for that very thing.

Her Words

For all of her coming across as an eccentric, darling little old lady, she is just as sharp of a box of nails. We share a deep love of history and politics, and she and I can get into discussions about things that happened twenty or thirty years ago; she has not forgotten a thing. We will talk for, like, ninety minutes about books that we've read, and she will go back to books that she's read twenty years ago.

We had a very unusual family growing up, I think. There was a lot of intellectual activity going on. Maybe it came from my grandfather on my father's side, who was German and would have big boxes of books shipped in. He would open a crate in the living room and you would grab whatever you wanted and needed, and that tradition continued up until my father died. Dad used to go down to Irv Coats's used bookstore, The Reader's Corner on Hillsborough Street, and come back with big grocery bags full of books and dump them on the dining room table. And you better get what you wanted because Dad read very quickly. Basically, he would read page by page while most of us read word by word. He'd be done with all these books in maybe a week or two and then he'd go and collect another bag of books to take and sell back to Irv's. We found out that we were buying and selling the same books back and forth because we hadn't all read them. And so actually, just before Dad died, we took the technique of putting these little red sticker dots in the front of the books, so we could say, "Oh, yeah! We've had that one before..."

My mother is anachronistic now. She is one of this whole generation of women like her who are gone, like Dottie Streb, who used to keep a gun in the ice box "just in case." Dottie was Old South and her family came from Kentucky. I can remember going to dinner at Dottie Streb's house. We were sitting at this beautifully polished table with the family silverware and China. In the crystal glasses there was some wine, and Dottie said, "You got to try some really great moonshine that I have." She went in the kitchen, she got a mason jar, she pulled out more of the family crystal, and she poured the moonshine into the family crystal for all of us to drink at this wonderful dinner table.

The first time I ever went up to Warrenton with my mother, we were driving, and she saw this old house on the hill and she says, "Well, that's where my friend so-and-so lived and I'm going to go in and say hello. I think her mother's still there."

And I said, "Oh, Mom, they're never going to remember you."

She pulled up in the driveway, and she went up the steps and knocked on the door. The door opened, and this little old lady said, "Douglas! Welcome back!"

I was born in 1957 in Sumter, South Carolina. I think they had been down there maybe a year. My mother always says there are two major dates in Southern history. One is the end of the Civil War and one is the invention of air conditioning, and I do believe she's absolutely right. The only way that you get the economic boom of "The New South" is if you get air conditioning so the Yankees can come down and be cool. Before then I lived in un-air-conditioned homes in the South in the summer, and it ain't fun.

Probably why she has never gone back to Sumter, and why she will never go, was that you got the Sunday *New York Times* on Wednesday, if you were willing to drive down to Columbia to get it, and you would go into the grocery store and they would put Klan rally materials in your bag, so you could go and stand up against Communism and Liberalism and all that good stuff, and integration.

When they moved there, she dutifully went to the big Presbyterian church in Sumter and volunteered like the good Presbyterian daughter that she was. My grandfather was Episcopalian, and my grandmother told my grandfather that she would attend the Episcopal church only after Douglas was safely raised Presbyterian. My mother moved out of the house; my grandmother started attending the Episcopal church with my grandfather.

And so my mother went and volunteered, and they gave her a Sunday school class to teach. They gave here the Sunday school materials to use. She read through them and she went back to the minister and said. "I do not feel like I can teach this material because I do not believe that God made white babies better than black babies. That is what is being taught here, and I can't do it. "

He thanked my mother very much for her offer to volunteer and as far as I know, she was essentially, at that point, de-churched and was shunned by the church.

I did not appreciate their courage until I went and lived in Hartsville, South Carolina, which is about forty miles away, a town of about the same size. It isn't the end of the world but you sure can see it from there.

In Hartsville there were ten thousand people and sixty churches. And that is not an exaggeration. Ten thousand people and sixty churches, and only about four or five of them were mainline churches, the Catholic church of course and then three or four standard Protestant, you know, the Episcopal, Presbyterian, and the Methodist. And then of course the First Baptist church. Everything else is warehouse churches in Harstville when I was there in '82 and '83, and that was a small enough town that everybody knew everybody's business. You sneezed on one end of town and someone on the other end of town gave you their handkerchief.

I appreciate now the absolute balls of a brass monkey it took for my mother to say that because she had been in small Southern towns. She had grown up in small Southern towns and probably knew precisely at that time that she went to that minister, what she was risking in terms of her social standing. And she was new in town. She didn't know anybody. That was her way to learn about people, to be part of that social circle. But she had the spine, the guts, the balls, the *chutzpah*—whatever you want to call it—to walk in and have the courage of her convictions to say, "I'm not doing this" in a town that is putting Klan material in your grocery bags, where everybody— God and everybody—knows what you're up to. I suspect that was part of the motivation for the visit my father received when he was a foreman at this factory.

Mr. President

And you have to understand as well what was happening in the South in terms of racial tensions then. We're talking about times that there was an Atlanta, Georgia, bus driver who shot a black veteran who was in uniform after having come back from fighting, shot him dead in the middle of the street in Atlanta because he would not sit in the back of the bus, and that was in the late '40s. There was a documented case where two black men in uniform were chased down by whites and killed. Emmett Till was not an unusual story. Emmett Till was only unusual only because his mother said, "I'm going to have an open casket funeral so they can see what they did." And that's part of what sparked so much awareness in the North, the pictures in *Look* magazine of the mangled face of Emmett Till in that coffin.

I did get out of watching my father and my mother growing up that, whatever you wanted to do, if you worked hard at it, you could get it done. We were encouraged to fulfill our passions. I am probably in many ways the least talented person in my family, and I say that with all love and charity. It's not a knock on me. It's not a knock on them. My passion growing up was history and politics. I was never laughed at or mocked for doing that or going out every election in front of

Precinct Two at Fred Olds School, handing stuff out. Nobody ever made fun of me for doing that.

Most of my interest in history is trying to figure out why a group of people would commit treason and would go to war for the right to own a person with the same rights as trying to own a chair. And in many ways, Southerners have not reconciled that history. It is still "moonlight and magnolia" when they think about it. My mother grew up in an era where *Gone With the Wind* was taught in history class. I came from an aristocracy that was built on slave labor.

There was a long time of my life that I didn't feel very Southern. I worked to get rid of my accent. But as I get older, I feel more and more that I'm Southern. I work at a different clock speed. I have a certain etiquette that others don't have, I find. I can remember my grandfather jamming me in the ribs with his elbows to make me stand when a woman entered the room. You said "Ma'am" and "Sir." I got a contract once because I escorted somebody to the elevator after we had spent a day with him. All of my colleagues from up North had already delved back into their laptops and email. But as the guy got onto the elevator, he turned around and said, "It's nice to find somebody who has old style manners."

Mr. President

Being Southern actually helped us be successful in Austria, because the South was basically kind of a monarchy. Austria was very caste oriented, very class oriented, lost a war—hey, sounds familiar—was occupied—hey, sounds familiar—and was still sort of looking back into the past glories of the Hapsburgs even as we were looking into the past glories of "Moonlight and Magnolia." In many ways, the atmospherics of living in Austria were like the atmospherics of living in the South in the 1960s.

I wound up in music school because I didn't speak fifth year Latin or Greek or French. I just happened to be a decent trumpet player and I was able to get into a *musik gymnasium* and studied trumpet for several years before going off and studying voice at The North Carolina School of the Arts.

My trumpet teacher was a blazingly cruel man. He was everything that you would expect. He was the first trumpet in the philharmonic and his dad had been the first trumpeter in the philharmonic, so it always came easy to him. I remember coming home and telling my brother Michael, "God, he's such an asshole. He's got to be a Nazi." Many years later, when the philharmonic had awarded him for his service to music, it came out that he actually had been a Nazi. And he was

307

a real true believer to the point that he had twenty-seven of his colleagues deported from the orchestra and they all died. And yet, through the years, after the war, everybody just moved on. So he still continued to play in the orchestra with people who knew what he had done, and he still continued to play for American Jewish conductors like Leonard Bernstein and played good Jewish music like Mahler.

I'm sure that he saw me, this American with this last name that was German, and many expatriate Jews were moving back at the time and assumed that I was one and took his feelings about that out on me as well.

We were given lots of latitude in our lives. I spent two years going in and getting myself into Vienna every morning, by myself, going to school until noon or one and then going to "standing room" at the opera and then getting myself home from downtown Vienna at midnight, back up to the house in Kritzendorf at one o'clock in the morning, and then getting up at five or six in the umorning and starting all over again—doing all of that unaccompanied. It's something that people would now call "free-range parenting" and shudder that they would let a child of that age do something like that. "How dare you risk their life and limb?" But for us it was like, "Here's your ticket. There's your briefcase. Go on and do it."

Somewhere or other, I found the materials for School of the Arts. In early '75, found a voice teacher because I was singing in chorus and enjoyed that, and I had a decent voice for a child my age. I put together an audition tape and sent in the tape and waited anxiously, because of course this was before any sort of computers.

We were in Europe during Watergate, and *Doonesbury* provided at that time the same sort of accurate news with withering satire that somebody like Samantha Bee or Jon Stewart provides now. So we got *The Stars & Stripes* and *The International Herald Tribune*, which was mashed a little bit to cover up what was going on, because it's international and you don't want to make Americans look bad. If you really wanted to find out what was going on, you read *Doonesbury*.

There was a character, Joanie Caucus, who was applying to law school at the same time that I was applying to School of the Arts, and there was a cartoon about a week before I got my notice that was Joanie and the African American woman who was her best friend. They both applied to law school together, and they got the envelope. I think Joanie's friend opened it up. Joanie was very, very afraid of it. And her friend said, "Relax, babe, you're in."

About a week later, I got off the bus. I hadn't gone to the opera that night. And Mom met me down at a plaza in Klosterneuburg that is a bus stop for all the buses in the neighborhood. There was a coffeehouse called Veitz that had an open porch where you could sit. So we got there, and she had the letter. I couldn't open it, so she opened it and she looked at me and said, "Relax, babe, you're in." That was how I found out about going to School of the Arts.

My grandparents picked me up at RDU. I stayed with my grandparents that summer and stayed some with Joel at Kilgore Avenue and then went to School of the Arts that fall. For a year I was in School of the Arts by myself, except for my grandparents and Joel. At that point School of the Arts was much smaller than it is now in terms of its campus. It was a compact campus in what was a shady side of town, so there's no going anywhere. I was there for three years and I was around some very talented people who were very driven and realized I was very interested in what I was studied but I was not talented enough to do it.

Looking at my brothers' drive and creativity, they were reflexive about that in the same way that my father was and the same way that my mother is. My mother can no more not be creative than Dad could or Joel could or Michael. And me, I was much more interested in how it all linked together. I was much more interested in musicology than music theory. I was much more interested in the history of opera than opera. I was much more interested in putting the opera together than learning the music. I figured out that there are a bunch of mediocre baritones there, and as a director I could actually be paid to learn about all this stuff.

I remember coming home from school the year my mother opened the shop and walking into the living room, which is where she had the first rack of clothes, and saying, "What's going on?"

"Well, we just went into business." I was eighteen at the time.

I spent a semester at NC State making up credits. Then there was the summer I went to Chapel Hill, and the following summer I worked for Mom. I worked in the shop. And, I don't know, I guess Mom always sort of assumed I knew how things were arranged, but I never really had a firm grasp of pricing of things, that this rack was this amount and that rack was that amount. And Mom didn't know that I did not know this.

It was a good six or seven months after I stopped working that she discovered the way I was pricing things was that I would stand at the counter and see what type of car people drove up in. If it was a fancy car I would charge them more, and if it wasn't a fancy car I would charge them less. I was renting $15 costumes out for $35 if I saw the guys drive up in a Mercedes, but if they drove up in a VW Bug, man, it was going for $15.

And I learned early on too that retail was not for me. It takes a very special person to do retail and it takes a real special person to do this type of retail this long. I was the youngest son. I knew my father as a writer. I never knew him as a job-holder, as a "wage slave," shall we say. So from Mom, I really got a respect for the small shop owner and what they've got to do and realized a) that ain't for me and b) just an enormous amount of respect for anybody who can keep any concern going, let alone anything as specialized as this was.

When my wife Anne and I were dating in 1980, I was living in South Carolina, going to graduate school. Anne was still living in Chapel Hill, and Mom, being the good mother-in-law-to-be wanted to get acquainted with the next to "join," shall we say. she called Anne up out-of-the-blue one day. And my mother said, "Anne, I'm coming over to

Chapel Hill with a large chicken. Would you like lunch?"

Anne said that, in that space and time, so many visuals went through her mind. If you see the picture of that chicken standing on the corner of West Johnson Street, the chicken with the squeaky cane and the tin cup, that's actually Anne in the chicken suit. That's the chicken that Mom was bringing over.

But Anne went by the shop after that and she and Mom were laughing about the story. I don't know how Anne came to offer to model the suit, but Anne modelled the suit and that picture was taken on the corner of Johnson and St. Mary's at the old house, which was still the first shop. Anne has laughed over that story for years, as have I and as has Mom.

We lived in LA—"we" being me and Anne— from 1991 to 1995. My wife worked for a motion picture and television fund, and she was the CEO of the foundation, so that was probably was the template for what would become Obamacare. That was a healthcare organization for people who had worked in the industry for a particular amount of time. You used to hear it called "the rest home in Woodland Hills" but it was a hospital. It was a cutting-edge Alzheimer's unit that pioneered a lot of the Alzheimer's treatment that's being used today.

One of her donors was the assistant to Edith Head, a great movie costumer, and there was going to be an exhibit of Edith Head's personal costume collection. It was like things like the *Breakfast at Tiffany's* dress. Anne arranged for Mom to have a private showing with this woman, and Mom loves Edith Head.

I worked for a bank at the time, and I took time off from work to take Mom around town. I took her to Musso and Frank's, which is this classic old Hollywood place. She was in a black dress with a little bolo jacket and white pearls, and I was in my banker outfit, gray slacks and sport coat and blue shirt. I don't think I had a tie. And directly across the street was Frederick's of Hollywood which is four stories of lingerie to entice the young ladies of Omaha. This was in '94, long before Victoria's Secret. If you wanted anything other than "granny panties," you ordered them through the mail from Frederick's of Hollywood, who advertised they would deliver it to you in a discreet brown package.

And she said, "Well, Son, let's go take a look. I'd love to go in."

So, fine. We went into Frederick's of Hollywood. At midday. In July.

Mr. President

The place was crawling with tourists, and of course people from all across the country wanted to get "delicates" for their wives and for themselves. We walked in and there was a sign that said, "History of Lingerie Downstairs in the Basement." So Mom said, "Well, I have to go see that." And we went down.

It was a long, narrow hallway with glass cases on either side, sort of an L-shaped gallery with the undergarments that Marie Antoinette wore on one side, something from Mary Todd Lincoln on the other, just all these historical things all the way, undergarments and what Russian brassieres looked like at the time, which of course fascinated my mother because she did not know they made brassieres in a different manner.

Well, the place was packed. I mean, people were in their flip-flops and their walking shorts and their Panama Jack shirts, and you could barely fit a sheet of paper in this place it was so crowded with all these people. And then came Tennessee-Williams-me with my mother, and Mom stood in front of each one of these cases and looked and commented on a few things and, as I said, was exceptionally interested in the Soviet undergarments.

We got to the place just where the gallery turned. Right at the end of the "L" was the

Madonna "Blonde Ambition." With the propeller tits. And my mother looked at that and she turned around and she said—and you know, she'd gone a little deaf at this point, so she was speaking louder—"Son, have you ever seen a titty-tassel dancer?"

And I stopped. How do you answer that? *Yeah, Mom, I go to the strip clubs all the time!* I looked at her and I said, "You know, Mom, I don't think that I have."

Thing had slowed down in our part of the neighborhood at this point. People were spending a lot more time at whatever case they happened to be in front of. Ears were pricking up.

And she said, "Well, I'll tell you that when we lived in Charlotte, your Aunt Jane and your Uncle Don and your father and I went to the state fair, and we went and we saw a titty-tassel show..."

"Oh, yeah, that's real interesting, Mom..."

Everyone had stopped and everyone was listening. Nobody was going anywhere. I was trying to pull on Mom's sleeve to get her to move a little faster—that ain't happening.

And she looked at me and she said, "You know something, Son? They can get those tassels on the top spinning in one direction and the tassel on the bottom going in the other, all at the same time..."

Mr. President

"Oh, really, Mom! Fascinating! I never knew that…" Now really pulling hard on her sleeve to get her to move. But she was not going anywhere, nor was anybody else.

"And you know that when we got home that night, your Aunt Jane and I nearly threw our backs out, trying to do that."

Finally, I was able to get her out. I'm sure that somewhere in Lincoln, Nebraska, there's somebody telling the flipside of that. It was years later she finally figured out how they did it. It's just by a threading on the screws—pun intended.

From my mother and my father both, one of the things that all three of us, my brothers and I, got was that we take people as they are and as they come to us. Dad could talk to anybody at any level. My mother is the same way. She didn't have to take in murderers from the Women's Prison. But she did. And she treated them with the same graciousness and respect that she would have treated some Old Raleigh person from the Garden Club.

She's lived her faith probably as strongly as anybody I know. That is why she was always taking women parolees into the shop to work for her so that she could help get them back on her feet. She always felt to a certain degree comfortable with them because she had grown up around my grandfather's prison labor and had known them and knew how the prison worked. But she had a steady stream of people who were, you know, the Women's Prison would place them in her shop as a way to get them to reintegrate into society. And she has done things for people that we will probably find out when they show up at her funeral and tell us the story. She has done stuff for people under the table, around the table, at key points in their lives when they absolutely needed something, a helping hand. She was somebody who lived "the good Samaritan" story. All the time.

Growing up, I think we use to laugh a little bit. We had called it her picking up another stray cat somewhere. But that was the callowness of youth. And she will never tell you about it. She's very modest about it. She doesn't brag about it, doesn't beat the drum. We may never find out about it. She made people of all stripes, ilk, comfortable in her shop. I expect you will have a massive contingent of Raleigh's drag queen population at her funeral.

In fact, Mom took me to see *La Cage Aux Folles* when it came out. Mom called and said, "Son, there is this really funny movie that we just have to go see." And she told me about it. It was after Dad had died, so I was still at Carolina. It was at

318

the Colony movie house, and I was the only heterosexual in line. With my mother. And I don't know why she did this, what she was doing or what she needed me to do this for, but she went, "Son, could you hold my purse for me?"

I'm standing there, in line at the Colony Theater to see *La Cage Aux Folles*, holding a purse, standing with his mother, so of course I fit right in. And she asked me to get something out of her purse and I reached in her purse and start rummaging around and—*pat, pat, pat, pat.* Oh, gosh, there's something heavy and steel here. And I patted around a little more. "Holy crap! It's a .45!" My mother was carrying this .45 in her purse. I said, "Mom, you've got a gun in your purse? Thank God I didn't hit the trigger!"

And she said, "Well, Son, it's not loaded…"

Chapter Nineteen
A True Matriarch

Becky Hanner, Willard's daughter, says, when she first moved to Raleigh, North Carolina, that North Hills Drive, now a major thoroughfare and site of a posh shopping center, used to be just a dirt road.

"You sound like one of those old Californian women," says her son Logan, who breaks into a crackly voiced caricature, the standard Katherine Hepburn impression from her later years, "This used to all be orange groves, far as the eye can see…"

When I met Logan, Doug's grandson, he was a pleasantly rebellious teenager working Saturdays at Raleigh Creative Costumes. Sitting now in his mother's living room, he is a grown man working in chemical engineering. His wife Heather periodically steps away from the circle of our chairs to check on their two sons. Logan's beard has not grown quite so long or dark as that of his brother Corey, seven years younger, who completes our circle with his girlfriend.

"How Southern do you feel?" I ask the room. They have all grown up in North Carolina and definitely qualify as natives, but it is a different kind of South than the one in which Doug herself was raised.

"One hundred and ten percent!" Logan boasts. His wife laughs. Heather is a Southern woman from a Southern family and deeper roots in the culture than her husband. Corey offers a more conservative twenty-five percent, but Heather says she considers her brother-in-law more Southern than her husband.

Corey asks, "Well, how are you defining being Southern?"

I say that I'm not really asking how Southern you are. I want to know how Southern you feel. But to give the issue more structure, I turn it toward something easily quantifiable and highly telling—Southern cuisine. Thinking of an Ohio girl I dated whose face scrunched up violently upon one sip of what local restaurants served, I ask, "Do you drink sweet tea?" In the North or Midwest, iced tea would always be served unsweetened.

Immediately the heads start shaking. Corey used to drink sweet tea when he was younger but not any longer. For all of his "one hundred and ten percent," Logan does not drink sweet tea.

A True Matriarch

Then there are grits, the ground cornmeal boiled as a hot breakfast cereal similar to oatmeal or cream of wheat, but more often savory instead of sweet, sometimes served with cheese. Corey eats grits. Logan does as well, but Heather quickly points to his use of non-traditional ingredients, such as sun-dried tomatoes, moving the grits more toward their Italian cousin, polenta.

All head nods when I ask about collard greens, but Becky points out that, when she was little, her family would eat spinach or Swiss chard instead, not Southern at all. The standard offerings of her transplanted household also included "lobstah." Sometimes she would open the refrigerator to find a one looking back at her, swaying its claws in the chilled air. Yes, they had to be kept alive, she says, because you have to cook them alive, dunking the lobster into boiling water head-first and hearing the "scream" as hot steam escapes out of the shell. "Through their butts," says Logan.

Even arriving in Raleigh at four years old, it was clear to Becky and her kindergarten classmates that she was different from them. She spoke with a different accent and continued to do so as she grew up and continued to feel that she was not a Southerner until she married a Southern man, Logan and Corey's father, at the age of twenty. His big, warm Southern family embraced her, literally as well as figuratively. "They are huggers," Becky says. Her parents were not. Doug later told Becky of how she would feel Willard tense up when she affectionately rested a hand upon the small of his back as she passed him by.

Becky was twenty-four when Willard and Doug married. He did not announce their impending nuptials to his children. At a party thrown by Wat to celebrate the couple's engagement, Becky's friend Anne Johnson asked her, "Aren't you so excited?" and she had no idea for what.

That following Christmas, Willard and Doug brought their children together to celebrate, with some initial awkwardness. Becky recalls that at one point, Doug prompted her son John to relate a particular anecdote and he declined, saying, "That's really a story just for family." But where Doug's prompting may not have brought their families together, her gifting did. She placed water guns in every stocking. Willard's children and Doug's children, grown and mostly-grown, spent the day running around the house, shooting each other, and starting to feel a bit more like a single, slightly-damp family.

Willard passed away before Corey was born, so he carries no memories of his grandfather. Logan remembers Willard saying, "I never 'worked' a day in my life." It was all play to him, no matter how serious the science. But Logan suspects that other memories of Willard may just be stories he made up in his head while looking at old photographs, like one that Willard took of himself appearing to fight a taxidermied bear that he found on a trip out West.

"Where's Awfulich?" Becky asks at the mention of Willard's travels.

"Awfulich?" I say.

I'm told he is a puppet as they begin to search the room. A plush black bear appears but is dismissed. That is a different gift from a different journey of Willard's. Heather knows just where to find Awfulich though, up the stairs where her sons have dragged him in their play.

So the puppet joins our circle. Named Ivan Awfulich—a joke, "I've-an-awful-itch"—Willard brought him back from a visit to Russia. Awfulich's molded plastic head bears the face of a smiling older man. A ring of golden doll hair encircles his baldness and a matching moustache and beard trail down his fabric chest. Awfulich wears traditional Russian peasant garb, an embroidered tunic over brown pants tucked into comically oversized boots.

Willard carried a box of red-inked ball-point pens with him on that trip. His hosts were overjoyed at the gift. Ironically, red pens were not locally available in Soviet Russia, and the novelty was a real hit. He returned with Awfulich.

But it was Doug who brought Awfulich to life, giving the puppet a voice and personality. None of the Hanners there can recreate any of Awfulich's antics or voice for me. Doug's performance of a Russian accent is apparently inimitable, affected as it is by her own. Looking at them smile at Awfulich though and knowing Doug, I can imagine the puppet coming to life in her hand, gruff and polite and maybe a bit confused by our local customs, his enormous boots bouncing along the top of a dining room table after lunch has been cleared on a Sunday afternoon.

Logan and Corey both made trips of their own to Austria with their "Oma," Doug. They remember seeing castles and playing with the Seifs. Helmut and Dora, who had looked after Doug's sons on her first visit, had children of their own near in age to Doug's grandchildren. And now those children are having children too.

On Logan's first trip to Europe with Doug, when Corey was too young to go along, Logan remembers stopping in London to visit Michael, who worked for Sony at the time, and Sony provided a car whenever Michael needed to take them around the city. Logan says these were very nice cars, Rolls Royces and the like, a luxury that he now realizes he was too young to appreciate.

Both of the Hanner boys worked at Raleigh Creative Costumes but at different times and different locations, Logan at St. Mary's Street and Corey at Hillsborough Street. Logan loved his time at the shop, dressing up as something different every day. Corey hated it. At thirteen-years old, he would have much rather spent his summer playing video games than being told to clean this and clean that, spraying down costume pieces that couldn't be laundered.

Still, he also felt a fascination for the shop when he first saw it. "Any costume you could imagine wanting, all you have to do is just reach out your hand and have it," he said—top hats, bunny suits, including the bunny suit that Logan wore to hide eggs for the younger children one Easter. "It was probably full of spiders," said Corey. "I didn't spray it very well."

The Hanners came to celebrate Easter at Doug's house on Lake Gaston, which she purchased with her inheritance from Willard after his death. Becky says that Doug intended the lake house as a kind of neutral territory where the various branches of Willard's estranged family, his children from different marriages, would be able to come together. The lake house came to be known as "Doug's Digs," and the wooden shield-shaped sign with that name painted on it which stood at the lake house now rests against a tree in the back yard of Doug's home. Doug had to sell the lake house some time ago.

It came furnished, not only with furniture but with a pontoon boat. Becky remembers the first summer they had Doug's Digs the family went out there to celebrate Fourth of July, and it happened to be one of the coldest summers on record, so cold that everyone on the lake had to bundle up for their celebrations. Doug wore her long trench coat as she took the pontoon boat out for the first time, and Becky remembers her looking like Mr. Toad from *A Wind in the Willows* with her long coat fluttering behind her, grinning broadly as the pontoon boat buzzed along the waves. Doug's thick-rimmed glasses must have completed the picture, appearing almost like a pair of old-timey motorist's goggles.

Out at the lake house, Easter celebrations included a big Easter egg hunt, with big Easter eggs. "Always L'eggs eggs," says Becky. The large egg-shaped plastic containers for L'eggs brand pantyhose held a lot more candy than regular egg-sized plastic eggs. The hunt expanded across the house, its yard, and the attached dock, even the pontoon boat itself, except for one year when a duck had made its nest on the deck. Doug had discovered a broom left outside picked clean of every one of its straw bristles. The duck had nipped them all away to build its nest from the broom's head. So actual eggs were on hand year, and the children had to be told to keep their distance. The lake's otters did not do the same, however, and each morning Doug's family noticed fewer and fewer eggs in the duck's nest as they disappeared to become an otter's breakfast.

And then there was burning Barney in effigy at the lake house. "Barn burning," quips Logan.

"Oh, that's good," says Becky.

Doug's shop never owned a Barney costume. But it did have a costume for a purple character named Hildegard the Hippo. As Becky puts it, "Doug is a woman who knows something about copyright law." She had been married to an author and to an inventor who held numerous patents, so she had a sense of how to navigate these issues. If anyone called to ask, "Do you have a Barney the Dinosaur costume?" She would say, "No." But if someone wanted to rent Hildegard the Hippo and tell their children this was Barney the Dinosaur, that was up to them.

In the late 1990s, those with the rights to Barney the Dinosaur won a case against the manufacturers of the Hildegard the Hippo costume and then began searching for and suing any shop that had Hildegard the Hippo available for rent, including Raleigh Creative Costumes. Naturally, they sued for just enough that it would cost less to settle out of court than fight the accusation, and the money received from all these costumers, as Becky tells it, funded the 1998 film *Barney's Great Adventure: The Movie*.

Although Corey was a fan of Barney the Dinosaur when he was little, Becky brought him in on the family grudge against the character and taught him their re-writing of his theme song, "I hate you. You hate me. I'm going to take your money..." Doug's family and friends would burn Barney in effigy at the lake house. On one Fourth of July, everyone in attendance at Doug's Digs received a piece of a Barney the Dinosaur cardboard puzzle that they ceremoniously tossed into a fire, one by one, bringing them together as a family this time against a common enemy.

"How would you describe Doug?" I ask.

Logan says, "A living time capsule." Corey agrees. You could ask Doug any question on any time period and be rewarded with a rich and satisfying answer.

A True Matriarch

"She's got a lot of fight in her too," Logan continues, and he relates story from the time Doug and Ben were living in Sumter. Doug was teaching Sunday school classes at the local church, and they complained to her that she was not teaching the proper lesson. She was telling the children that God created all races as equal, and Doug would not bend on that principle. Instead of teaching white supremacy, she quit.

"She is a true matriarch," Becky says. "Doug reaches out and takes people into her fold." Not only did she build relationships between her own children and Willard's, and between Willard's children and Willard's other children, Doug created an extended family of connections among those she brought into Raleigh Creative Costumes. Becky remarks on how many high school students found at the shop a place to be themselves and also to practice developing a little bit of responsibility, and sometimes these were hard to find in other areas of these teen's lives. And then there was the work that Doug did with the Women's Prison and the women recently released from prison whom Doug offered a job when few others might give them a chance.

"And, Doug didn't have any brothers or sisters herself," Becky points out, "She was an only child."

Her Words

So it may have been that Doug did not grow up in a large family, but she made one.

Chapter Twenty
Yes, You Can Wash Gorilla Hands

Raleigh Creative Costumes closed in 2007, and on its last day former employees from across the years came to raise a glass and say good-bye.

<u>Ruth Bicket</u>

I was Doug's first model. In 1975, Joel and I and a couple of other people would go out to wherever we could figure out to go, in costume, and pretty much wear a sandwich board advertising Raleigh Creative Costumes. He and I were buds and lived in the same commune. We are a day apart in birth and both hail from Warrenton.

My roommate Jeanie, who married Joel, she was terrified of meeting Doug. She had heard all the "dragon lady" stories from Joel. We were both terrified. I met Doug probably in '73 or '74, when she and Ben came back from Europe. It was such a revelation. I love this woman. And I've loved her ever since—her warmth, her stories, the fact that she and I both grew up in Warrenton and our ancestors had been relatives and best friends. My great aunt and Doug's mother had been bosom buddies.

I kept hounding her for a job, and, lucky me, she picked me up. I started full-time I guess in '79. I was the first paid employee. The shop was on West Johnson, around the corner from St. Mary's, a little old Victorian house. I loved it. I absolutely just dug on it.

I was into theater. I had done costuming and acting at Theater in the Park and Raleigh Little Theater, and I had wanted to work here in the shop since its inception. It was just where I wanted to be, and I felt so at home from my very first day. And I loved the little Victorian house.

I guess I was full-time until about '91, when I started developing problems with the bod. Something called Reflexive Dystrophy Syndrome developed in my left arm, and I'm left-handed. The docs said, "Just bow out for a while," and I did that. I came back to work off-and-on through the '90s, and I came back in 2002 for Halloween and stayed through Easter.

Jimmy Thiem was so lovely, such a wonderful guy. He taught me all about Old Raleigh. Doug had done a pretty good job of it, but from Jimmy I learned from Victorian times on. It was a great history lesson. And I loved him very much. I still miss him. His son and I knew each other before. We were both hippies together, so I knew him from about the time I was twenty-one.

I had run away with the circus early on, Ringling Bros. and Barnum & Bailey, and had been an aerial ballet dancer. A couple of years after I started at the shop, the circus was in town, and I remembered some of the people who were still in the circus family. So Doug and I went out to Dorton Arena, where the circus always performed, and looked for the people that I knew. We ended up back in the costume department and were feeling the costumes. All of a sudden, these several men in suits came up to us and said, "Ladies, follow us." We were busted by the Ringling Bros. costume police. And we were sat in this room that was surrounded by windows with drapes for several hours. They kept poking through curtains, looking at us. Apparently, they decided we were just a couple of crazy women, and they finally let us fly, fly away.

Her Words

Betty Mittag

I think I probably would have been her second employee. Ruth was working there. And of course it was in that little shop on West Johnson Street, where that office was—I guess it used to be the porch—and there was like a chest there, and when I went into the shop, I had to jump on the chest, through the window to go into the shop. I was probably about forty. I think I worked for Doug seventeen years.

The first Halloween there, I remember, it was such a zoo. And the daughter of a friend of Doug's was working there and her boyfriend was working there, and I was supposed to be doing office work. The boyfriend had been there was week or two. I didn't have any idea what the kid's name was, and I had to write him a check. So I said, "Doug, what is his name?" Doug didn't know either.

Doug always worked so hard. And she found her people. One of the things that used to drive me crazy was Doug wanted her employees to be informed. They would come in late with their breakfast and sit down and read the newspaper. And Doug would be out there working her butt off, and it would drive me crazy. It used to drive me crazy.

A True Matriarch

She was always very kind and caring, but on the other hand, she could be tough too. I remember Doug being the angriest I ever saw her when she shipped Michael's piano to London on Flying Tiger Airlines, and Michael, I think, sold it. I never, ever saw Doug that angry. And you know, Doug is very, very, very Southern, but, boy, was she angry with him—just cold anger is all I can say, on the phone.

I had read Ben's book, *The House of Christina.* I read that book and really loved it before I ever came to work for Doug. I always thought the title for the book about the shop that I liked the best was the one that June came up with, "Yes, You Can Wash Gorilla Hands."

We probably had the most fun the time we took a cow costume and went to Warrenton, and somebody up there that Doug knew had a Bentley, and we went all over town with a cow costume. We did historic Warrenton, and we had a wonderful time, June and Doug and I.

You heard about the Jimmy Thiem drawer? "The Jimmy Thiem Ladies Afternoon Society" or something, we called it. And we would have a shot of bourbon. We did that because at his funeral because we just didn't think it was Jimmy deserved. It just wasn't enough. So we all came back to the shop and said this just wasn't what we should have done for Jimmy. So Doug ran up to Cameron Village and got a bottle of bourbon and we all said a toast to Jimmy.

And then, of course, there was Suzie the murderess. Doug volunteered at Woman's Prison, and she hired Suzie. She had poisoned her husband, and one of my favorite things about Suzie was you couldn't discuss legal abortion with Suzie. That was murder.

Once there was a fellow who came in after Halloween and specifically asked to speak to me. I worked on the floor a lot too. It's a small shop. Everyone does it. And he thanked me. He was very gracious. He thanked me because I dressed him as a female for Halloween, and he came out of the closet. When he came to see me, it was as a woman, and he thanked me for being so kind to him that he had the confidence to come out of the closet. I'd had no idea. But when he came in, he had these lovely nails, and he'd done a lot of work. He'd done a lot of work. And he was very kind.

A True Matriarch

<u>Josephine Evans-Gibson and Christine Evans</u>

Josephine: We graduated in '85 from Broughton High School. That was an after school, work-release program. You go to school half a day and then work half a day. Doug was with that program. They was on St. Mary's Street, and Broughton was just down the street from the costume shop. All we had to do from school was just walk to the shop.

Christine: Actually, it was the Wake County Commissioner's office, because they had that program that year. We did a commercial for them, advertising for businesses to hire teens, and we had a spot that summer on TV, with the costume shop, being advertised. We were famous for a little while there. People would see us on the street and say, "Oh, we saw you on TV!" because they ran it the whole summer long. We were the first to be hired. It was something that we wanted to do, get started in the world of "responsibility." And this was a good place to start.

Because this was my very first job, I had to learn everything, but it was kind of exciting. I'm a history buff. I like history. So I kind of found it fascinating when I first found out about all the different time periods to dress people. I never knew people wore this type of clothes for this type of time period, being young and never being exposed to anything like that. So it was exciting, because I could tell people, "Oh, you wear this in this time period, and I think this would look good for you for this time period..."

I'm thinking about the fashion-type way, how things are now versus how they were then. Fashion is revolving. Because we worked in the costume shop, we could say, "Oh, we remember when we saw that kind of fashion back in the day," when we would talk with different people about fashion. And when I see people, I say, "Oh, my first job was at a costume shop."

And they are like, "Wow. Really?" So they think that is fascinating. I tell them some of the stories of what happened and how we would dress people and what sort of make-up they would need to put on. It was neat. It was really neat.

Josephine: She taught us a whole lot about history.

Christine: Yes, she did. She was very nice. Very nice. Very nice. She welcomed us with opened arms in training us in what we needed to do to provide people with the help they needed when they came here for costumes. She trained us quite well. And she was very patient, being that we were young, didn't know anything about costuming or make-up of that sort. She was very patient with us in that.

Josephine: I didn't know any more than what Christine had told me about all the people she had met and all the different kinds of stuff that was in here and all the people she had helped—how people were when they came in, how she couldn't believe people was asking for certain types of things we had never heard of, like a boa, the feather boa. We had never heard of that or what you would do with that until Doug told us what it was and everything, what you would do with it. And she would show us books with all the different time periods, and that would give us an idea further of what you would do with it. And as we went along, we got real creative ourselves in how we would try to dress people up. And if we was unsure about it, she always had enough material up in the shop. She would show us, "This is what you need to put with this and put with that..."

Our first Halloween was a nightmare. When I say, literally a nightmare, because, you know, it was Halloween. We were so tired. It was just standing room. It wasn't hardly even standing room because everybody had waited until last minute. "Could you put me in this? Could you put me in this?" Everybody was trying to pick something up at one time. And then other people were coming in, asking for stuff they couldn't find other places. So we was all tired. We were all tired, and being that was our first Halloween, we were like, "Wow. Is it like this all the time? Every Halloween?"

And Doug said, "Yes." The next year, we knew what to expect, but that first one, our tongues were hanging out.

Our parents were very supportive. They didn't have a problem with us going to school and working, because we were home at a decent hour. The shop closed at 9 during the Halloween season and during the regular hours it was 5 or 6. Then we were still able to do our homework and still do our work. So it worked out very well. We worked here a little bit after graduation and then after that we went to college, so about eighteen or nineteen.

Christine: Doug was very personable. She would always like to know about how everybody in your family was doing. Some places you work at, they could care less about people's families. She was very generous, of course, during

Christmas. It was in her nature to want to see everybody be happy.

At the time our parents had died, my mother actually, we were in college and Doug found out about it. She was very supportive and she gave good words of encouragement, and things like that when we were going through a—you know—a tough time. We were only nineteen. So I would say she's a very personable person.

June Merrow

In 1976 and in 1965, the 200th anniversary of the town of Willsboro, NY, a town of about 1,800 people, I organized and did research and gathered vintage costumes for this pageant. We found that people had very old costumes which they were happy to have shown. And these costumes hadn't crashed, even though they had not been preserved in acid-free boxes the way they should have been.

It was just terribly exciting. Magnificent costumes came out of people's closets, even 1776 men's coat from Paris. We had a ball for 800 people wearing these costumes, and it just transformed the town. One thing I noticed when, for instance, I was walking into the grocery store, and a couple of these ladies went by with these sweeping skirts and their tiny waists, was the wistful look on the face of an old man who remembered when women dressed that way.

My husband was given a job here in North Carolina by my daughter and her husband in the field of gas chromatography, isolating toxins in ambient air. So I was happy to come down. My daughter is also highly into fashion and design.

When Doug was first down at St. Mary's street, my daughter went to get an Egyptian costume for her son's school performance. The shop was just a house then, and the way it was set up, you had to sort of jump over a box and go through a window to get into it, and there was a little curtain in one corner where people pushed that aside and changed, maybe more than one.

My daughter Holly was fascinated. She said, "You know, my mother should work here. She loves costumes, and she's done some of this stuff."

So the next day, I went down, and Doug hired me on the spot. Doug is my type of person—whimsical, loves to laugh, never missed a chance to laugh. And disorganized, like me. Just my type of person. I don't know if I've ever talked to her when I haven't ended with a laugh, because that's the type of person she is. And she's the type who sees the cup half-full, and "What's next? What's next?"

A True Matriarch

I think I was known at the shop for being very over-the-top and very picky, and I've lived long enough so I knew the history of some of these costumes because I had known people who wore them way, way back in time. I did a good Wyatt Earp and Doc Holliday, because when I was twenty-one I had a sort of a crush on this old, old man who was a cowboy from the West. He had abandoned that way of life and had become a foreman on a ranch in Montana and was very well known as Rattlesnake Ed because he had killed so many rattlesnakes since they killed cattle and horses. He was a friend of my fathers, and that was how I got to know him.

One day, he said, "Would you like to see my journal?"

And I said, "I surely would." And he opened it up and he showed me, "Now here is a letter from Virgil Earp. I knew Virgil and the boys." He was the most romantic figure.

I worked at Raleigh Creative Costumes for twenty-four years. And we just enjoyed our customers so much. We met people from all over the world, and we got into the spirit of things. We frequently dressed in costumes because we were just, all of us, immersed in how things had changed and how styles come back about every twenty-five years. They keep coming back and coming back, which is always fascinating to me.

I will never forget this one pair of people who came in. The lady was blonde, enormously obese, with the most beautiful gold earrings, and she rented a red-fringed flapper dress in about a 4X. She was "a lady of a certain age," probably about sixty-five, and I realized that the man sitting the chair in the area where she was pirouetting was her husband, but there was something very creepy about him because he looked as though he was not real. He was so old that I feared that if I were to brush by him that he was going to fall dead, literally. So between the two of them, my eyes were bulging.

She just wanted a photograph—maybe for a Christmas card—of herself as a gun moll of the '20s, shooting probably a rum runner. She rented the costume for $50 or $60, went out, had the picture taken, brought it back, handed it to us, and then she stripped off her earrings and gave us her beautiful earrings. They were waterfall earrings of gold beads. It just made my day. They were wonderful.

A True Matriarch

David Serxner

Doug and Ben were some of the first people my mother and my father met when we first moved to North Carolina from New York. Stan couldn't find a job up in New York, so he got a job down here at Shaw. He had been active in theater, and we got involved with Raleigh Little Theater, and Doug found out Mother could sew. That's all she wrote. That really was all she wrote. We've known them since.

It had to have been since 1967 because I think the first show that Mother did was *Midsummer Night's Dream*. I was born in '65. Mother said I had just been captivated by Doug's accent. You know, I didn't speak much English at home. I spoke Dutch, because Mother is Dutch, and I was apparently captivated by Doug's accent. The story is that, the word "bottle" in Dutch is *fles*, and I said, "flaaayyyse."

I was in and out when we were on West Johnson Street. I remember Doug lending me Roman soldiers when I was in sixth grade. By then Mother had stopped working. She got the books set up, got them settled into West Johnson Street, and then stayed for a year or so after that. Then she found them Betty Mittag because we all belonged to Temple Beth Or.

And it was funny, because I started working for the shop in 1980 when I was in high school. We were on St. Mary's Street. We had moved into the Siddell Building by 1980.

I think, one of two things, either I needed a Halloween costume or I had been cast as the brother in *Miracle Worker* and they didn't have it in the budget at Enloe High School to get me a costume, so we got it from the shop. But I got the costume I needed, and I returned it to Doug. It was Halloween, and I was given a tape measure, and that's it.

There have been times I have worked at the shop and gotten paid. There are times when I have worked and have not gotten paid. There are times I have come in and wound up working and not gotten paid and not cared. I told Doug, "I'll take this book in exchange." And when I went into business for myself, the deal was that I would pull everything I needed and do all the alterations and get it cleaned and pay a nominal fee, or I could work and it would be a trade. That ended up being really good for me, to work it out as a trade. And then when I worked at Capital Opera, we were supposed to store our stuff here and rent it through the shop and build up credit like that, but that never worked out for various reasons that I just can't start to fathom.

A True Matriarch

But when I started dealing with opera singers, I just didn't want to deal with the general public anymore. See, the opera singers, I can control them. Pins, baby. Pins. "You want some pins in that crotch? You want to suddenly discover that the rough side is suddenly on the inside next to your precious skin and not on the outside?" I remember the opera singer I had to tell, "You must wear underwear."

You know, my mother used to make all my clothes when I was a child, and when I would grow out of them, they came to the shop—my Peter Pan costume, my Indian costume. The pink harem girls, my mother made. Those things would had to have been built in '77 and we were renting them out until I took them away in May of '06. They are at Dixie Trail now. I said they needed to come home, because more than likely she made them in the dining room at Dixie Trail anyway. And we actually still have one of the caps. Those we patterned on *yarmulkes* because it was for a Temple Beth Or and Beth Meyer Synagogue combined Saturday night entertainment evening. They had three belly dancers. It was my mother, Sharon Zagray, and somebody else. I don't remember who. I'd ask Mother, but I'd be afraid she'd kill me.

Her Words

Freda Holloman

I had a six-week class in high school, where they do the little electives-type things. That was about all the sewing I'd ever done. I'd always put together costumes for my boys growing up, but I'd never done much sewing. I mean, I knew how to sew a button and, you know, that kind of thing, on, but as far as really sewing, it was never a big thing.

I actually got the job at the Magic Corner when I used to do stunts, so to speak, for my husband's birthday every year. I always came up with some kind of creative thing, and I went to rent a fat suit that the Magic Corner had, so I could strip for him for that birthday, out of the fat suit. I did Marilyn with a plastic butt and a fan on the deck so it would blow the skirt. I did Cher with three boobs. That was when she was advertising all that Equal stuff, and I told him it was from all that Equal.

When I went to take the costume back, I had noticed that they had in the paper for part time work, so I said, "I that sounds interesting." I'd retired, so to speak, from fourteen years sitting behind a desk, doing bookkeeping and accounts payable with the comptroller for a wholesale distributer. I thought, "Well, that would be a totally different aspect from what I had done," and they hired me. Then years later, the Magic Corner closed, and I came to Raleigh Creative Costumes.

I kind of really taught myself how to do the things that needed to be done. If I had something that needed to be done and played with it a while and didn't feel I could accomplish it, then I'd come to Doug. Otherwise I'd do what I could do and then say, "Hey, see what I did!" She was always bragging on me, you know, how creative I was and talented I was. I didn't feel like I was that way at all. I've never felt that I've been that much of a seamstress.

But I was so in awe of her knowledge and the retaining of the information that she had. I'd be good to remember lunch, and she's telling all these things, and all the talents in her friends and in her family and in herself.

And she's watched me go through a lot of things, a lot of changes. She's gone through all of my surgeries, all of my mom's surgeries. Then there was the time I fell off the ladder. I was in the men's department over on Saint Mary's Street. I think we were actually changing the round things a little bit. When I came back down the ladder, I missed the last rung, and reached back to catch myself and caught myself on that little pinky. I come out, holding my little pinky, and it was straight back at a 45-degree angle. And

I was like, "Miss Doug, I think I may have broken my finger."

And she looked at me and she said, "Do you have a doctor we can take you to?"

"What do you mean, do I have a doctor?" So she took me and put me in her van and took me over to, I think it might have been her nephew over there off of Computer Drive, down from North Hills. He took one look at it, and he was like, "I'm not messing with that," because he didn't know if the tendons or something were messed up in it as well, so we had to go to an orthopedic place. And she took me over there.

Meanwhile, I was trying to hold ice to this finger that's at this forty-five-degree angle, and she was like, "Are you ok?"

And I was like, "Yes?"

We walked in. He took x-rays, pulled it out, wrapped it up, and I went to work the next day.

I actually got a tip once. I had a guy that came in fairly late on Halloween night. We were still open for a little while, and he wanted to be a pirate. This was actually before the *Pirates of the Carribbean* movies. Of course all the good stuff, by that time, is gone, so I was just running around, just everywhere, trying to find something. This was a really cute guy for one, probably in his late twenties, and I was thinking I'd hate to send him out there in this rag when he could really make a good pirate. So I was finding all this stuff, and he gave me a fifteen-dollar tip and would not take the change back from what I charged him.

He said, "No, you have worked so hard, and I feel so good in what I have on," and he would not take that money back. The rental itself was like $50. I was floored. And he wasn't drunk. You're thinking, late Halloween night, most of them are going to be drunk. He was not drunk.

Then of course, there was the old lady—or the older lady—who used to come in every Halloween, wanting to be as skimpy as she could be.. So we'd all go back there, trying to find what little piece of material we could make some kind of costume out of that she could still get away with wearing. "Short and sexy! Short and sexy!" And she had to be, I don't know, at least mid-fifties then, but every year she'd come in, "What you got in short and sexy?" We even sold her the Fembot from the *Austin Powers* movie, that negligee that was see-through except for the little puff ball brassiere. She bought the Fembot.

Her Words

Onia Morgan-Royster

The first thing I have to start off with is that Doug's grandfather delivered me, in Oxford, NC, so Doug and I have this joke that he delivered me to her. And it was amazing. We were just talking and she stated that she was from Oxford, and I said, "A Taylor delivered me."

She said, "What Taylor?"

I said, "W. Taylor."

She said, "Oh, that's my grandfather! He delivered you to me!"

I first met Doug while I was in prison. I was going out to different churches. The Presbyterian ministry was what sponsored the prison chapter at RCCW. That's the Raleigh Correctional Center for Women. I had met Doug in church one Sunday, and the chaplain mentioned to her that I was being released soon and would need employment. But before I had gotten released, Miles Wright, who was another member of West Raleigh Presbyterian church, he offered me a job and he owned this pre-press company called Eyebeam, which was right around the corner. But I didn't have any experience in what he needed, so after six months, we decided this wasn't the job for me.

I went on and worked for Raleigh Lions Club, and they did a lot of sewing. They had a contract with the Army, so they did a lot of sewing. So when I had gotten released, I saw Miss Doug again, and she had stated that she wanted to hire me. So, okay, she owns a costume shop, I'm thinking she wants to hire me as a seamstress, but she said, "No, I don't need you to sew. I need you to be my bookkeeper," because she had known I had a degree in business management.

So I was like, ah, this woman wants to hire me. I was out of prison less than a year. And she wanted to give me this chance. I started March 27 of 2001. And you know the old saying, once you work at a costume shop, you're here for life. Even though I went on to other jobs—because at that time we had lost our insurance here and she knew I needed a job with benefits—I still worked here part-time.

But it's like there's a connection here. Miss Doug, has been like a mother to me, a best friend to me. And once you get in her fold, it's like you're a big family, because anything that impacted anybody else that worked in the costume shop, Miss Doug would get on that phone and call up everybody or she would send out an email. Having her in my life has truly been a blessing.

Even when I was at my other job, on days when I would feel stressed, I would get in my car and come here to just sit, you know, or come here and work. This was the place that I could just come here and be me, because you didn't have to be any type of person but yourself here. You didn't have to go into business mode. You didn't have to be politically correct here. You just be yourself. And that was the beauty of it. I know that's what I'm going to miss the most, just leave work "I'm going to go to the costume shop and hang out."

My first day—this was when we were at St. Mary's Street—that first day was so weird because I was the only black person working at the shop, but the employees that were there were Freda and Betty and Bob. I mean, they just treated me... It was like you walked in to an extended version of your family.

And I remember I was going to Shaw. I was still continuing to go to Shaw to finish up another degree, and my final semester, I thought I would have to drop out. I was living on my own. I had to work but I wanted to go to school too, and the classes they offered were all in the daytime. And I didn't have a license then, so I would have to leave work, and maybe take a bus. I would be gone for five hours out of that day before I got back to work, and I knew that I couldn't live like that. So I was thinking about having to find another job, a night job or something, when Miss Doug made sure that someone was there every day to take me to school and someone was there to pick me back up when my class was up, so I wouldn't lose all those hours. I would just lose maybe an hour and fifteen minutes out of work. So I tell everybody, she helped me get this last degree because I could not have gotten it without her. And this was an everyday thing. She made sure that either Betty would take me or Bob would take me or she would take me. God knows that's amazing.

And any time I needed extra money, I would say, "Miss Doug, I need to work extra hours." I could come in the evening time or on Saturdays.

It's just, I mean, I would take a bullet for Miss Doug. That's just how real it is. I could not love her any more if we had the same blood running in our veins. When I say, "That's my mother," I really say that's my mother because that's how I look at her. She has nurtured me over the years. Any endeavor I ever pursued, she was always there. When I graduated, she was there. When I had events at my other job, she was there. She always showed up. The only thing she needed was an invitation, and she was there. And you know, that makes a lot of difference.

She was one of those persons that continues to be a constant in your life. She's not there just for a season. That's the beauty of it. That's why even when I changed my job, I would come here any time she needed me. I'd work on Saturdays and Sundays, but I would do it ten times for her.

I brought my clients here to work. One of my clients that she hired, she hired last year as a seamstress. The program I work with now is Glory, Glory House of Refuge, and we are a transitional housing program for single homeless women who are infected with HIV and which is maybe also compacted with substance abuse issues and mental health issues. And, you know, when you are dealing with women who are HIV-positive, they think their lives is over with already, so they have very low self-esteem.

But Doug hires the people that no one else would give a chance to. She will bank on you, and I think that's that Christian love she has in her. She don't judge a person by their past or by their appearance. She just finds the genuine good in a person, and she builds on that.

There is one particular lady that I referred her to Miss Doug, and Miss Doug said, "If she wants to tell people that she is HIV-positive, that is her choice. If she don't, it doesn't make a difference." And they formed their own bond over the years.

When Doug said she needed help, I brought my girls. And I said, "Y'all not getting paid. You're just coming to volunteer."

But by the end of the day, Miss Doug pulled me aside. She said, "Onia, how much do you think I should pay?"

And I said, "Miss Doug, they come to volunteer."

Miss Doug said, "Oh, no, no, I want to pay them something." And that's just the person she is. She is just awesome. And when I tell people, I say, "Miss Doug is over 75-years old and she get around better than I do." And she do!

I told you I was in prison. When I got out, I was on parole, and Betty Mittag, the former officer manager, her son Jeremy was my parole officer. I found all that out when I came to work for Miss Doug. It was like we were meant to meet each other!

When I came to work, and Miss Doug kept on saying, "Jeremy and Betty..."

And I said, "Miss Doug, that was my PO!"

She said, "I told you, you was meant to be here!"

So, yeah, I could sit here and talk for hours and tell you about the things that she has done and the way her life has impacted me, and it would take that long because, I mean, it's been a little over six years that I have been knowing her, but it seems like a lifetime.

Her Words

This is the same woman who, when she went out of town to New Mexico, I was the one she gave the keys to her house and said, "Go check on my house every day." She made me feel like all is forgiven. That's a blessing.

Epilogue

The last time I saw Doug before I went off to grad school, I came down to her new home at *Rue Sans Familie* to drop off my cell phone with her, which wouldn't function in London. It was my first time seeing the new place with its close-packed houses, tight roads, and total absence of sidewalks, a neighborhood custom-built for retirees to look out for each other so they could live with independence, *sans familie*—"without family."

Doug welcomed me at the door and ushered me past a gingerbread-like wooden case displaying Austrian figurines and the silver set that had been buried in the garden when the Union Army approached Warrenton. We sat and I showed her the phone and how to work it. And she asked what I thought I might do with all those hours of interviews we'd recorded. I said I didn't know. I had no clear idea of what would be the best use of those stories, only that I felt a great comfort knowing I had them saved. A cardboard box full of those tapes would remain stored at my parents' house until I began the transcription process some seven years later.

As we talked about my intended adventure, she was reminded of another story from her I told her that there was a girl in Wales with whom I'd been corresponding for about two years and convinced myself that I was in love with. So I studied what I could of Wales in preparation for her magically returning my feelings and wanting me to join her there in her native land. As part of my research, I'd watched the 1941 film and winner of that year's Oscar for Best Picture, *How Green Was My Valley*, about the lives of Welsh miners in the nineteenth century, and this reminded Doug of another story

She saw that movie as a young girl. It was playing at the Colony theater, later renamed the Rialto, the same theater where she took John to see *La Cage Aux Folles* with a pistol in her handbag.

In 1941, the United States had not yet joined the fighting of the Second World War, but we were aiding the Allies in their efforts with financial support. In North Carolina, that meant inviting the British Royal Navy to train and rest here, housing their troops, whom we gave space in Raleigh's Umstead Park to set up tents. Doug's parents had taken some of the British soldiers with them to see the movie, a bit of that good ol' Southern hospitality at work.

To the British, North Carolina had what amounted to a tropical climate, so the men went about in the same sort of gear you might see them wear in their imperial colonies of India and Africa, khaki uniforms with shorts that stopped above the knee. Doug said she had never seen a grown man in short pants before. She had also never seen a grown man cry, and as they left the Colony after *How Green Was My Valley*, one of the soldiers who had come from Wales quietly wept for his far-away home.

As soon as she finished speaking, I told Doug that story was great and I wished I'd been recording it. She said she was sure I'd get good use of it somehow. I was going to be a writer, after all, and she understood from Ben how mysterious and unpredictable an author's creative process might be.

I think she must have also known, without having to say it, that just having in your heart and mind the stories of your people, the people who come from where you came from and lived where you now live, or really just any people, the real stories of real lives, enriches the spirit. Doug offers that enrichment freely for just about any ear that will hear.

While in the UK, I never met that Welsh girl, but I did get a visit from an old costume shop co-worker who was touring England with his wife, seeking historical material to support his work with the Raleigh Renaissance Faire. Of course we chatted a bit about how Doug was doing when we'd each last seen her, what the latest was we'd heard about, and I talked about these interviews I'd taken with her, stories like the Un-Reconstructed Nazi. I thought he might have heard mention of them before since he'd worked with her longer than me, but I was surprised to find his expression blank in response. That's when it occurred to me that a person might see Doug on a daily basis for years and still not have uncovered the particular anecdotes I had recorded with her. The value of these stories to others began to make itself apparent.

In the following years, I found Doug had gifted me with this very versatile conversational resource to rely upon, particularly when the topic turned toward Southern culture or the history of North Carolina, to the evolution of race relations and Civil Rights issues—as the election of America's first black president highlighted—or toward the impact of Research Triangle Park on the cities of Raleigh and Durham and the town of Chapel Hill, how the influx of "Damn Yankees" and "carpetbaggers" made the home I grew up in different from the rest of the South, from the rest of North Carolina.

I know now how IBM used to stand for "I'm Bein' Moved" when I think about childhood friends who appeared in my neighborhood when I was seven-years old only to be sent off again four years later. I look at how much more sushi than barbeque I ate as a teenager and, in college, how much more espresso I drank than sweet tea; instead of observing these changes from the Raleigh in which my mother grew up with fear that we are losing our Southern culture, I remember Doug's words, "There's a lot that we are getting over."

And I know that there are so many more stories that I have not captured and will not capture, so many more people that I could speak to and even more with whom I cannot speak, who have passed on before this project even began. But like my friend who, for all his years of knowing Doug had never heard before heard of the Un-Reconstructed Nazi, I know that there are many out there for whom these stories that I have managed to put together make-up a hidden history in which they may find as much meaning in as I have. So although these stories you have read could be more, I am thankful they are not less.

May they make more sense of your world, as they have mine. May you never receive a visitation from the White Citizen's Council. May your potatoes be only ever cooked the exact right amount of time, not half a minute more or less. And remember, if someone speaks to you and you realize you don't know their name, just say, "Aw, Cuddin'!" and drop your handkerchief as you mumble something that sounds like it could be their name, because there's a very good chance that we are all related anyway.

About the Co-Author

J. Griffin Hughes was born, raised, and currently resides in North Carolina's Raleigh-Durham area. He studied theater under Doug's former costume shop business partner Sue Scarborough and worked on and off at Raleigh Creative Costumes from 1998 to 2007 before receiving his graduate degree in creative writing from Royal Holloway, University of London. For more information, visit jgriffinhughes.com.

Made in the USA
Middletown, DE
23 July 2018